D0099226

ALSO BY STANTON E. SAMENOW, PH.D.:

Inside the Criminal Mind

CO-AUTHORED WITH

SAMUEL YOCHELSON, M.D.:

The Criminal Personality: A Profile for Change

The Criminal Personality: The Change Process

The Criminal Personality: The Drug User

BEFORE
IT'S
TOO
LATE

STANTON E. SAMENOW, PH.D.

BEFORE
IT'S
TOO
LATE

WHY SOME KIDS GET INTO TROUBLE—
AND WHAT PARENTS CAN DO ABOUT IT

TIMES 𝕿 BOOKS

RANDOM HOUSE

Copyright © 1989 by Stanton E. Samenow, Ph. D.

All rights reserved under International and Pan-American Copyright Conventions.
Published in the United States by Times Books, a division of Random House,
Inc., New York, and simultaneously in Canada by Random House of Canada
Limited, Toronto.

Library of Congress Cataloging-in-Publication Data
Samenow, Stanton E.
  Before it's too late.
  Bibliography: p.
  Includes index.
  1. Problem children—United States.   2. Child rearing—United States.
  3. Juvenile delinquency—United States—Prevention.   4. Deviant behavior.
I. Title.
HQ773.S215 1989   362.7'4'0973   88-40163
ISBN 0-8129-1646-8

Designed by Ann Gold
Manufactured in the United States of America

9   8

TO MY MOTHER,
SYLVIA L. SAMENOW,
FOR HER HELP WITH THIS BOOK

A NOTE TO
THE READER

Like all children, the antisocial child requires much love, patience, and compassion. The assumption often is made that a youngster becomes delinquent because he was not nurtured adequately—that he is a product of uncaring, indifferent, and irresponsible parents.

In families where the parents are unloving and otherwise inadequate, the children *are* likely to experience a variety of difficulties, but not all of these children turn to crime. Most of the mothers and fathers who have consulted me have demonstrated a profound capacity to love. That love has been tested repeatedly by a child whose self-appraisal is not based on being cherished by his parents or on his own constructive achievements, but rather on getting away with that which is forbidden and, to him, highly exciting. Warm and loving though his environment may be, he grows increasingly restless, disagreeable, and disobedient. As the years pass, he becomes destructive to himself and others.

Parents of antisocial children feel bewildered and helpless as their offspring reject their guidance and, eventually, become lawbreakers. Many of these mothers and fathers have declared that they would make virtually any sacrifice to help their child become self-disciplined, constructive, and happy. They are heartsick at being reduced to ineffective bystanders as their offspring throws away his life. Undeservedly, the parents of these children brand themselves as failures.

This book may seem tough, even harsh in its tone and approach. I say little about affection, warmth, and a nurturing attitude. What I emphasize is that parents of antisocial children must combine with love and caring, stern measures that, at times, are at odds with their own concepts of good parenting. My objective in writing the book has been to communicate what it takes for a parent to institute a tough—yet loving—approach that can assist this particular type of child in developing an enduring sense of self-worth and self-respect.

CONTENTS

BEFORE
IT'S
TOO
LATE

INTRODUCTION

Upon starting this book, you, the reader, may wonder if you are encountering one more psychologist who blames parents for the misbehavior of their offspring. The answer is emphatically *no!* My central premise is that children become antisocial by choice: lying, fighting, stealing, and other forms of destructive behavior are willful acts.

But parents can take steps to prevent antisocial behavior from developing into an entrenched pattern. If a child is regularly manifesting such behavior, it may not be too late for corrective action. Before taking preventive or corrective measures, however, it is essential that parents fully understand what is involved.

Although few people would dispute the importance of preventing antisocial behavior, a heated controversy rages about whether prevention can or should be undertaken if it entails identifying children at risk when they are quite young. In the first chapter, I shall discuss this issue: Is the possibility of misidentifying children sufficient reason to place a complete moratorium on early identification and prevention? Afterward I shall discuss extreme manifestations of antisocial patterns. This will provide the reader with a frame of reference for my use of the term *antisocial* throughout the rest of the book. Parents will find help in identifying specific forerunners of antisocial behavior in chapters 2 through 8. They will learn that a difference does exist between a phase of development or occasional, relatively innocuous misconduct, and a *pattern* of behavior that should serve as a red flag to those involved in rearing the child. Once early manifestations of antisocial behavior are recognized, it is possible to work toward preventing these from becoming fixed patterns.

Subsequent chapters will focus on errors that parents and others make as they encounter the forerunners of antisocial behavior. Here the emphasis is upon both prevention and remediation. In these chapters, I offer guidance to parents about how to help their children modify and eliminate behavior that shows signs of becoming increasingly destructive to themselves and others early on. To parents with older children who are displaying entrenched patterns of antisocial behavior, I offer suggestions to help them cope more effectively. It may be tempting to skip immediately to the suggested remedial measures. But to do so would be as inadvisable as a surgeon's cutting into a patient before studying anatomy and physiology. In fact, it is vitally important to know exactly what requires correction, and why, before one tries to take such action.

As any person who has raised a child knows, children make choices from the time they are very young. The toddler chooses whether or not to obey parental orders forbidding him to touch valuable household possessions. The child who has knocked over a lamp chooses whether or not to admit that he did it or to blame the cat. As time passes, the choices become more numerous and complex. Parents are often wrongly faulted for *causing* a child's irresponsible behavior, when it is the child himself who made the choice.

What of the role of the environment in shaping behavior? A recognition that children make choices does not mean that parents or other environmental forces are totally without influence. While the individual makes the choice, the environment can inhibit or promote choices in a particular direction. For example, lack of parental supervision makes it easier for a child to get away with misconduct. If a parent is present, the child is more easily restrained and guided. But even the twenty-four-hour presence of a parent does not guarantee that a child will stay out of trouble because it is the *child* who still makes the ultimate choice.

No conclusive evidence exists that can fully account for why children become antisocial. Every reader knows at least one family where both parents are loving, nurturing, sensible, and responsible—in short, outstanding role models. Their children internalize the norms and values to which they have been exposed and function responsibly—except for one wayward child. He rejects everything positive for which these role models stand. Explanations abound about why this happens, but nearly all of them are simply conjectures. Yet because we do not know what causes children to make certain choices does not mean that we must throw up our hands in despair and conclude that no useful guidance can be offered.

The human mind naturally tries to make sense of things, to explain why. The heredity-versus-environment controversy remains unresolved. Significantly, there is a growing awareness that environment does not play the critical role that many people have thought. Even Ann Landers, who has been advising readers for decades through her newspaper column, has said, "This is not to say that environment counts for nothing, but we now know it is less significant than we thought."[1]

If we don't know why a child is the way he is, let's say so and not invoke explanations that can turn into excuses and hinder constructive efforts to address problems. Even the discovery of the root cause of a pattern of behavior would not *ensure* our ability to eliminate or change it.

Much can be done by parents when they understand the errors in their children's thinking. I have observed that when parents are confronted by their offspring's antisocial behavior, *their own errors* in thinking and behavior interfere with their ability to embark on an effective course of action. The titles of chapters 10 through 15 describe errors in the ways parents think that may seem so self-explanatory that the reader may wonder if I am stating the obvious; yet what appears to be self-evident, even simple, is neither when a parent is caught in a maze of difficulties with a child who is manifesting patterns of antisocial behavior.

The majority of the parents who have consulted me were far from incompetent, negligent, or abusive. They were mothers and fathers who were confused, angry, sad, frantic, and guilt-ridden because their children were getting into increasingly serious trouble. These parents usually were candid about their own shortcomings, in many cases being unmercifully and unjustifiably critical of themselves. As might be expected, they did not seek consultation and help until they were having problems with their children that seemed overwhelming.

As I wrote this book, I drew upon detailed notes of my conversations with parents. In these notes were recorded the parents' reflections and assessments of their children as well as detailed descriptions of troubling incidents. In obtaining information, I have also had access to school reports and medical information. Frequently, I have had the opportunity to interview other family members, school personnel, social workers, counselors, and therapists whom the family previously consulted. A tremendous amount of information has been obtained from evaluating and counseling adult offenders and gaining access to reports that describe how they functioned during childhood. And, of course, of inestimable value as a source of information have been hundreds of interviews with youthful offenders whom I evaluate and counsel in my practice. In writing the book, I have changed all names and altered details that might be identifying of individuals.

All the information that I have gathered leads to one inescapable conclusion: Corrective measures must be taken as early as possible with the child who is already showing signs of heading in a direction that will bring him into repeated and increasingly serious conflict with the world around him.

Identifying a half-dozen errors made by parents (and others who regularly encounter such children) and suggesting corrective measures does not necessarily constitute a "cure" for all antisocial behavior. But parents should find effective the suggestions for recognizing and correcting their own errors as they struggle to help their child choose a different path. Parents can nurture, advise, discipline, and offer opportunities to their children. However, they cannot decide for a child what he wants in life. In the final analysis, it is the *youngster* who makes his own choices. We can only strive to do our very best to help him make informed and responsible choices.

PART I

THE EARLY IDENTIFICATION/ PREVENTION CONTROVERSY

1.

THE CHILD AS SHAPER
OF HIS OWN DESTINY

It seems that as far back as I can remember there have been alarm and despair over escalating juvenile crime. As a child in the 1950s, I heard radio reports about the mushrooming problems with youthful gangs in the big cities. When I was in high school, many of us read Evan Hunter's *Blackboard Jungle* or saw the 1955 movie based on his book, which graphically depicted teenage delinquency occurring right in the classroom, no longer confined to the streets.[1] In the 1960s, we began to hear about a surge of juvenile crime in areas that had been regarded as virtually crime free. In

11

suburbs as well as in the inner cities, youngsters were dropping out of school, using drugs, and committing crimes. In the 1970s and 1980s, juvenile court dockets became increasingly jammed with criminal cases. By 1981, nearly a half-million juveniles were under some form of correctional supervision.[2]

The first juvenile court, established in Illinois's Cook County in 1899, was designed "in a spirit of benevolent paternalism" and was devoid of the idea that "children were capable of criminal intent."[3] During the latter part of this century, juvenile courts that customarily provided social services in order to rehabilitate rather than punish lawbreakers were faced with an onslaught of children who were not simply wayward youths, but hardened repeat offenders.[4] Providing them with social services—requiring a brief stay in the detention center or lengthier incarceration in a juvenile correctional facility—had little, if any, impact on these youngsters. The persistent juvenile delinquent exhausted the resources of the juvenile justice system and continued to prey upon society. The 1980s have seen an increasingly desperate outcry for courts to take more extreme measures to contain juvenile crime, which is assuming ever more serious forms. A 1984 federal report asserted that ten years' experience with minimizing punishment and relying on prevention demonstrated that "this medicine has not produced a cure."[5] The emphasis on rehabilitation of repeat offenders that was prevalent in the 1960s and 1970s has given way to "get tough" policies. Citizens want these youngsters off the streets. More detention facilities have been constructed. Violent juvenile offenders who have been impervious to penalties imposed by the juvenile justice system are increasingly being handed over to courts where they must stand trial as adults. (All fifty states have provisions for trying certain types of juvenile offenders in adult courts.) And in 1987 the Supreme Court was being asked to rule on the power of the state to execute teenage murderers.

In my clinical practice, I see youngsters who are referred by juvenile courts, sent by school counselors, and in nearly all cases dragged unwillingly to me by their parents. For the most part, these boys and girls are already knee-deep in crime. As I evaluate them psychologically, I find that their defiance and excitement-seeking began as early as the pre-school years and that their criminality is far more extensive than anyone suspects. Their parents are overwhelmed by fear, anger, and guilt. Guilt can be the most devastating emotion, for it often paralyzes parents so that they are unable to take effective action. As they struggle to make sense of it all, the mothers and fathers of these youngsters are positive they must have done something horribly wrong that caused their children to become so irresponsible. But rarely is this the case.

It is tragic that for decades, psychiatrists, psychologists, social workers, and educators have convinced parents that they are chiefly responsible for shaping their children's destiny. Erroneously, the experts have asserted that the child comes into this world much like a totally unformed lump of clay and then is haplessly molded by parents. Millions of mothers and fathers have internalized this message and, understandably, feel blameworthy for everything that goes wrong.

Most of us assume the awesome responsibility for raising a child with a mixture of eagerness and apprehension. It is, after all, potentially the most exciting and fulfilling undertaking of our lives. How crushing the disappointment when we sense that we are losing control, that things are turning out far differently from what we had hoped. Certain that we are the ones who are failing, our confidence in our instincts and skills as parents falters. Convinced that we are to blame, we become angrier with ourselves than with our sons or daughters. But is such severe and unrelenting self-castigation justified? Are we in fact so totally responsible for our children's behavior?

The conventional wisdom claims that if a youngster has serious problems, the parents must be their source. This point of view has been consistent for decades. In 1942, Dr. David Levy stated, "Excessive mother love, indulgence, and overprotection of the child produce personality traits which lead to delinquent behavior."[6] In 1979, Dr. David Elkind said, "I have argued that middle-class delinquency is essentially a reaction to parental exploitation. Such a position clearly places the burden of blame for middle-class delinquency upon the parents."[7] And finally, in 1986, Ludwig L. Geismar and Katherine M. Wood pointed out, "Juvenile delinquency appears to occur disproportionately among children in 'unhappy homes' where there is poor communication; marital disharmony; [and] unaccepting, unaffectionate parents."[8]

Yet the daily experiences of millions of parents, as well as a relatively recent body of psychological research, indicate that the child is *not* a passive receptacle. Rather than haplessly being shaped by his surroundings, he himself shapes the behavior of others.[9] Two researchers in the field of child development have pointed out that any credible model of child development must take into account "the child as an active agent in social transactions."[10] Any parent of more than one child knows that children differ in temperament from birth. One infant may be fussy, irritable, and restless; another may be placid and contented. Isn't it natural for a parent to respond differently to a cranky, colicky baby than to a cooing, quiet one? Whereas most parents try to raise all children with love and to provide them equally with opportunities, they invariably treat each one differently. It could not be otherwise for, from birth, children have different temperaments, personalities, and needs.

But what does this have to do with crime? A lot, so far as identifying the source of the problem goes. If one were a fly on the wall of my office, one would hear juvenile offenders blame their parents and parents blame themselves for their youngsters' misconduct. As these boys and girls realize just how vulnerable their parents are to feelings of guilt, they level increasingly serious accusations against them. And so mothers and fathers who already doubt themselves as parents become even more guilt-ridden, depressed, and eventually even angry at each other. Some of the families that consult me have already visited other counselors or therapists, and if the parents didn't have enough problems before meeting with these professionals, they had more than enough afterward. This is because many well-meaning counselors and other mental health professionals are convinced that the cause of a child's bad behavior is bad parenting. I couldn't disagree more! Let's look at what goes on in most of the offices where these troubled families seek help.

When the youngster is interviewed, he is on the defensive in that he is being asked to account for his behavior. To exonerate himself and possibly to avoid an impending penalty, he deploys a variety of tactics. Besides minimizing the seriousness of what he has done or denying entirely that he has done anything wrong, he cases out the interviewer in order to figure out what that person wants to hear. There may indeed be problems in the family that the counselor identifies as having caused delinquent behavior. Aware that this is the counselor's perception, the child complains that the rancor among family members drove him to act up.[11] Overlooked is the possibility that the family ties have been weakened by the youngster's unrelenting belligerence, sneakiness, and untruthfulness.

Most youngsters know that they can gain a sympathetic ear by complaining of mistreatment at home. One boy asserted that his parents were so restrictive that they would not trust him to do anything on his own. He portrayed his mother and father as oppressive to the point of being smothering. The focus then shifted from his misconduct to the alleged overprotectiveness of his parents. What the youngster did not disclose was that at one time his parents *did* trust him, indeed still really wanted to trust him again. Not mentioned was the critical fact that his mother's and father's distrust developed in response to repeated incidents of his sneaking out of the house late at night, skipping school, and hanging around older youths who were getting into trouble.

In another case, a youngster told a counselor that he was a victim of child abuse. He described in unsparing detail how his mother lost control of herself, pushed him against the wall, and started knocking him around. His mother's behavior then became the focus of attention during the session rather than what he did to provoke her reaction. As it turned out, this mother had demonstrated remarkable self-control until that incident. For months, her son ignored household rules, failed to come home on time, and called her names when she tried to talk to him. Finally she became completely unnerved at two in the morning when he awakened her by wandering in drunk, yelling, and cursing.

In both situations, the youngsters felt exonerated because of the counselors' sympathetic reaction, and the parents were no closer to a solution; indeed, they felt even more distraught than they had felt before they sought professional help.

There are also those situations in which no specific conduct by the parent is singled out for censure. Instead, the counselor develops his own theory of family dynamics that he uses to explain and thereby inadvertently excuse the child's misbehavior. In one such case, parents of two adopted boys were told by a psychiatrist that it must be their unconscious resentment at not being able to have children of their own that played a role in one of the youngsters becoming incorrigible. Ignored was the fact that the other child, also adopted, was trustworthy, an honor student, and a delight to be around. Also ignored was the effort these conscientious parents had put forth to help the delinquent— only to be rebuffed at every turn. The erroneous assumption made in each of these instances, and in many others that I could cite, was that the parents were at fault.

In some of the cases I've evaluated, adversities not of the child's making do exist: divorce, alcoholism, poverty, neglect. It isn't surprising that policymakers and members of the helping professions have long regarded the juvenile delinquent as "the understandable product of his social environment."[12] (A former U.S. attorney general asserted, "The clear connection between poverty and the harvest of crime is manifest."[13]) Understandably, upon identifying negative environmental factors, many clinicians, educators, and court personnel regard delinquency as a normal or adaptive way for the child to cope. Professionals may believe that delinquent behavior represents only a neglected child's attempt to compensate for attention that he did not receive in other ways. Or they may reason that a child naturally turns to drugs when he is exposed repeatedly to his parents' drinking and pill taking to alleviate their own anxiety or depression.

It makes good theory perhaps to say that the child's personality unfolds in response to the people and events around him. In my experience, the cause-effect connection is not so simple. Of course, environment can affect behavior, but the longer I have been involved in research and clinical practice, the more I have been compelled to recognize an even more important fact: The environment from which a person comes is less crucial than the choice the individual makes as he responds to that environment.

Let's talk about the "latchkey child" who does not have anyone at home to supervise him after school. In one such case, a mother held two jobs to make ends meet. Her two boys did not see her until late in the evening. Because they had little direct parental supervision, it was not surprising to a social worker that one of the boys drifted out of the neighborhood, engaged in shoplifting, vandalized property, and finally was arrested as he was leaving a store concealing stolen merchandise. But before drawing any conclusions, let's examine the entire picture. This conscientious mother had made arrangements for the boys to go to a neighbor's home each day after school. There they were to do their homework, then play in the neighborhood. The mother would call each afternoon to talk to both boys. If the boys wanted to do anything out of the ordinary, they were to call her at work for permission. One of the boys never posed a problem. The other regarded the freedom inherent in the situation as license to do whatever he pleased. So here was a situation of two boys who grew up with the same mother, in the same home, in the same neighborhood, and who had the same opportunities and temptations. But each chose to react to his environment in a different manner.

One might argue that these children were not truly neglected, that others are cast adrift without any supervision. Let us consider such a case. When a social worker finally came to the dilapidated inner-city residence of two elementary school boys, she found no adults present in the squalid apartment. The only food in the refrigerator was a dry, hardened piece of chocolate cake. The boys were removed from this environment and placed together with an affluent foster family where the parents not only nurtured them as though they were their own sons but also provided superb opportunities for a first-rate education and cultural enrichment. Now the boys are adults—one is practicing law, the other is in the penitentiary convicted of a series of armed robberies. As I investigated the background of the latter, I discovered that he had received preferential treatment from his foster parents, in that more attention and money had been expended on him in a desperate and unsuccessful effort to help him change his increasingly antisocial patterns. The responsible brother required no extraordinary measures to motivate him to obtain an education and establish himself in a career. Here was a situation in which two brothers experienced the same severe deprivation, but responded in a radically different manner to subsequent opportunities.

In another case, a counselor assumed that a child turned to drugs because the parents had provided poor role models by drinking and using tranquilizers. It is difficult to dispute the desirability of a parent's integrity, perseverance, compassion, and other positive qualities. And yet every reader of this book probably knows of a family where the parents have been loving and responsible, but in which one of the offspring rejects those good role models to follow a path totally different from his siblings (who *do* pattern themselves after the parents). Conversely, I have known parents who are poor role models but whose child, instead of identifying with them, identifies with other people in his environment whom he admires. In one family, the father was in jail and two of the sons had been incarcerated. The mother was struggling to maintain her own emotional and financial stability. The youngest child in the family, when asked why she did not fashion her behavior after the antisocial role models prevalent both in her family and in the neighborhood, responded in three words: "I wasn't interested." She had observed the world around her and concluded that she would be like people who were doing something constructive with their lives.

The point I am emphasizing is that children *make choices.* Although they do not choose the environment in which they are raised, they do choose how to deal with it. Does this mean that I believe that what parents do has no impact on their children? Not at all! Most of us who are parents try to be good role models. It is important that we endeavor to practice what we preach. Usually our children internalize the values we endeavor to instill in them. But this happens by choice, not by passive absorption.

That children make choices might seem self-evident. But how often this simple fact is overlooked when they are in serious difficulty and people are casting around for explanations. There are children who make a series of choices *not* to live within legal, moral, or social bounds; they have contempt for rules and ignore others' expectations. What other youngsters thrive on, they find insufferably boring. In an interview, one such girl told me that the kids who attend classes and don't use drugs are ''missing out.'' For her, and others like her, life is most worth living when they are doing that which is forbidden.

The human mind desires to make sense of things. After the fact, mental health professionals are skilled at providing explanations. There is the gag that if you come early to your appointment with your therapist, you are anxious. If you come late, you are resistant. And if you come on time, you are compulsive. There are ready explanations for everything. But such explanations often are more clever than they are correct. And so it is with explaining delinquent behavior. We keep coming back to theories that have been accepted for decades. We say that it is the parents who are at fault. Or society at large that shuts children out of the mainstream, causing them to fail so that they commit crimes to achieve recognition. Or we claim that specific outside forces corrupt them, such as their peers, television, or the movies. But these theories explain little about origins or motives of antisocial behavior. Worse still, they are misleading, even dangerous, because everyone and everything becomes the culprit, *except the actual perpetrator of the crime.*

The much-cited role of peer pressure in criminal behavior is a prime example of the fallacious cause-effect reasoning that continues to be prevalent. Yes, peer pressure exists; it is an important aspect of life nearly from womb to tomb. And it is true that most children want to belong to a group. The pure, unvarnished truth is that people choose the company they keep. Children want to belong, but they choose the groups to which they want to belong. One father despairingly said to me that if his son saw two groups of kids, one that was talking about sports, rock music, and school and another that was speaking in profanities about teachers, discussing drug purchases and what girl was an easy mark, his son would invariably choose to be with the second group. In short, children do not get pressured haplessly into a life of crime. They make deliberate choices to do so!

At this point, the reader may believe that I am letting parents and society off the hook too easily. He may further conclude that while crime prevention is a desirable objective, I have written off societal efforts to achieve it. On the contrary. If I thought that society (parents especially) could do nothing preventive in this regard, there would be no reason to write this book.

I don't contend that a child's environment is completely irrelevant to his engaging in criminal conduct. There are certainly external conditions that either can inhibit or facilitate a person's inclination to break the law. If drugs are not available, a child will not become a drug addict. If stores fail to provide surveillance and do not press charges when a person shoplifts, more shoplifting will occur than if strict deterrent measures are taken. If parents ignore irresponsible behavior by their child, it is likely to persist. Yes, there are things that can be done. But, don't forget, it is the child who ultimately makes the choices.

This is an era in which personal responsibility is increasingly emphasized. In psychology and psychiatry, there has been a gradual trend away from relying on deterministic (psychoanalytic) concepts of human behavior and on remedial measures based on those concepts. Yet while currently much is said about holding people accountable for their behavior, whenever one reads about antisocial conduct, the inclination still is to place the locus of responsibility outside the individual. My objective in clinical work has been to help the antisocial individual change the way he thinks so that he will change the way he behaves. But in working with parents and children, I recognize that there are things parents can do *before* they reach that point of desperation at which they call upon outsiders such as police, courts, or therapists.

In no sense do I move away from my findings that irresponsible and criminal behavior are the results of choice. I do not blame parents for "producing" criminals because they may be deficient as parents. But I do recognize that there are errors parents make that could be avoided as they try to help their children become responsible citizens, errors that may in fact reinforce the behavior they wish to inhibit. I shall discuss these later.

My purpose in writing this book is to help parents recognize the forerunners of what could become an established pattern of antisocial conduct in their children. More specifically, I will identify and describe thinking patterns of children and their parents that underlie or facilitate antisocial behavior. Recognizing that parents cannot control many of the choices their children make, I shall recommend ways that they can foster a habit in their youngsters of making responsible choices.

I must make clear that I do *not* intend to label young children as criminals. Rather, just as we strive to identify early in life many types of problems (physical handicaps, learning disabilities, emotional problems), so too we ought to strive to identify and help children who are at risk of injuring others and causing untold misery both for themselves and others because of an undeveloped sense of responsibility.

2.

ANTISOCIAL THOUGHT AND BEHAVIOR —THE EXTREME CASE

Every child who steals a candy bar does not become a confirmed thief. Nor does every little kid who fibs become what some call a pathological liar. Even the most responsible youngster occasionally acts irresponsibly. Like other types of behavior, antisocial conduct occurs by degrees. Perhaps there *is* "larceny in every soul" or, as a former U.S. president said, "lust in every heart." But the larcenous thought of the youngster who contemplates stealing a candy bar is hardly comparable to the teenager who, in fact, has stolen nearly anything that is not bolted down. Similarly, there is a marked difference between the rare white lie told by a responsible person to avoid embarrassment and the incessant lying of the criminal who covers his tracks and calculatingly misrepresents himself in order to victimize innocent people.

Naturally it's important, in writing a book about antisocial tendencies in children, to avoid being an alarmist. It would be irresponsible of me to imply that every child who pilfers candy from a store, gets into a fight, makes a prank call, or fails to do well in school will develop into an antisocial human being. No matter how careful I have tried to be in the past, at least one or two reviewers have accused me of viewing most of the population as incipient criminals. These critics contend that virtually any reader can identify in himself patterns that I have described as "criminal." If it is a hazard to discuss confirmed adult antisocial personalities, the issue is far more sensitive when discussing incipient antisocial patterns in children. The *Diagnostic and Statistical Manual of Mental Disorders* of the American Psychiatric Association, often referred to as the bible of mental health professionals, is the standard reference for establishing such diagnostic criteria.[1] It flatly states that the diagnosis of "antisocial personality disorder" must not be applied to anyone under the age of eighteen. Instead, the term "conduct disorder" applies to children. In a sense, I do not disagree with the stance of the Psychiatric Association in that it could be damaging to declare that a child has an "antisocial personality." It takes time for personalities to gel, and it is important not to mislabel a juvenile in a manner that might be harmful. In fact, I have many quarrels with psychiatric labels. I abjure their use because they often conceal far more than they reveal and are open to misinterpretation. Never in a report to a court, school, or other agency have I written that a young child has an "antisocial personality." I describe instead how that child is functioning—how he behaves and perceives himself and the world.

Using the word *antisocial* as an adjective to characterize a certain type of child is not an unusual practice. Antisocial, as applied to juveniles, appears in newspaper accounts, books, and numerous other places in reference to boys and girls who either are incorrigible or who repeatedly break the law.[2] In this book, I am using the phrase *antisocial child* descriptively, not as a fixed diagnostic label.

Staying away from the use of stigmatizing labels is necessary. But to engage in denying the obvious—that young children *can* display antisocial patterns of behavior—can only lead to more serious problems later.

Before I discuss hallmarks by which parents can recognize developing antisocial patterns in their children, I believe it is essential to clarify what I mean by *antisocial thinking and behavior*. An understanding of full-blown antisocial patterns as they find expression in the career criminal will provide the reader with a frame of reference for what will follow.

You may have heard of the phenomenon called medical students' disease. This occurs when medical students, upon reading about a disease or condition, believe they have it. As you meet the criminal in this chapter, I hope you won't conclude prematurely that you, your children, or someone else close to you is a "criminal" based on recognition of a characteristic or two. I can't stress enough that irresponsibility and criminality occur *by degree* and that occasional irresponsibility does *not* a criminal make. It's a point I'll repeat throughout this book.

The criminal approaches the world with a sense of ownership, as though people and objects are mere pawns on his own personal chessboard. He aims to control other people just to enhance his own sense of power. Human relationships are avenues through which he pursues conquests and triumphs. The criminal expects others to do whatever he wants without hesitation. He delights in arguing for the sake of arguing. He is intent on winning what he regards as a battle, no matter how trivial the issue. He is a master at ferreting out weaknesses in others and ruthlessly capitalizing on them. When people oppose him, he can be merciless. Ignoring the rights of others, the criminal sounds like a constitutional lawyer whenever he believes that he has been unjustly treated. Nearly everything he does, he does to feel powerful.

The criminal is a loner. Although he associates with people whom he calls his friends, no one ever really knows him, not even his best buddy. By lying, he covers up his activities or tries to talk his way out of jams. Lying may take the form of a made-up story or alibi, but more often the criminal lies by omission as he leads people to believe they are getting the whole story whereas he is leaving out a great deal that is self-incriminating. He baffles people because he lies seemingly for no reason. But even lies that appear senseless do make sense when one understands his underlying motivation. Whenever the criminal believes he is pulling the wool over others' eyes, he feels he has the edge; every time he gets away with something, he finds it exciting.

The criminal takes from others, but rarely gives without an ulterior motive. Such a person does not know what trust, love, or loyalty are. If he can gain something for himself, he will betray his best buddy. A criminal may profess to love someone, but this turns out to be far more sentiment than substance. This person is so focused on pursuing his own immediate objectives that he does not care what others think, nor does he consider their feelings. Invariably, he hurts those who care most about him. In one way or another, a criminal's mother, father, brother, sister, spouse, and child all become his victims.

The criminal is unrealistic in his expectations of himself and the world. The responsible person is accustomed to coping with daily frustrations, setbacks, and disappointments. He knows Murphy's Law—anything that can go wrong will go wrong. The criminal, on the other hand, anticipates instant success with minimal effort. He expects the world to fall into line with his predetermined notions. For him, Murphy does not exist. If anything goes wrong, he invariably finds a scapegoat. Rather than assume responsibility for his poor performance, he quits the task at hand and blames other people.

To a criminal, life consists of a series of essentially

unrelated events in which he seeks immediate gain and a buildup. He plots and connives, but rarely plans. Psychologists have observed that the criminal lacks both the ability to learn from the past or the capacity to think long range. But this is untrue. He learns in areas that are of importance to him. If he believes he has messed up an opportunity, he learns from it and calculates the ways in which he can achieve his aim the next time. He may not map out a savings program for his family's future, but a crime can incubate in his mind for years until he finds a ripe opportunity to enact it.

Let me make it clear: The criminal knows right from wrong. He has a conscience, and he has strong fears about the consequences of being apprehended. But intent upon a course of action, the criminal reacts to these deterrents in a manner alien to most of us. He has the uncanny capacity to shut off both external fears and fears of conscience as instantaneously as one switches off a light. Because of this capacity, he changes from tears to ice in a flash. He can fervently pray at morning church services and an hour later thrust a gun in the face of a liquor store owner. When others hold him accountable, the criminal's excuses are limited only by his imagination. In ways both blatant and subtle, he claims to be a victim and tries to deflect attention from who the real victim is. This type of person spends a lifetime sizing up parents, teachers, employers, and the many others who take him to task. He becomes a master at figuring out what they want to hear and feeds them what he thinks they want to know. Often he is so persuasive that others let him off the hook.

What drives the criminal to act as he does? As I've

discussed, it is widely believed that adverse life circumstances (such as poverty, parental rejection, or lack of opportunity) or perhaps even a mental illness propel him into crime. But the simple fact is that this person is far more a victimizer than he is a victim. From an early age, the criminal has made choices to live as he does. He has long regarded as a living death a life that centers around family, community, school, and work. The criminal does not find sufficient excitement in socially acceptable outlets. Instead, he craves the high-voltage excitement that comes from doing the forbidden. To him, there is a far greater satisfaction in stealing a stereo than in earning the money to pay for it.

Despite this characterization of the criminal as thoroughly repugnant, he often comes across to others in a very different way, for he is likely to be intelligent, talented, and charming. A master of deception, he may also appear conscientious and even as representing the epitome of responsibility. Having made a good initial impression, he may be entrusted with a job with considerable authority. But recognition for legitimate accomplishments and opportunity to exercise power in the course of a day's work do not satisfy him. Thus a wealthy, powerful executive embezzles from his company, a security guard robs the place he is charged with protecting, or a minister siphons off church funds to pay for personal luxuries. Another pattern the criminal may follow is to earn a reputation as a dependable worker. His successful employment serves as a badge of respectability, and gives him room to get away with more outside the job.

With a winning personality, the criminal gains the trust and confidence of others and then preys upon them. People who believe they know him are incredulous when they discover that such a nice guy does such terrible things. The criminal counts on this; he knows that most people operate from a base of good will and trust. Time and again, he is helped by others' conviction that he is at heart not a bad person, but a good guy who is the way he is through no fault of his own. Those who sympathize most with him and give him the benefit of the doubt are among his chief victims.

Even the most cold-blooded criminal regards himself as being a decent person. If caught red-handed, he may acknowledge that he broke the law. The regrets that he expresses usually are over being caught, but occasionally they are over the crime itself. But no matter what he has done, within himself he believes that he is a good human being. The fact that he has a conscience, that he has done good deeds for others, that he has talents and skills, all contribute to his positive self-image. A man who had killed two police officers commented with complete sincerity that just because he murdered a couple of people, he was not a bad person.

As I've said, we all have probably detected some of these patterns in people whom we never would regard as criminals, perhaps finding some even in ourselves. In the criminal, all are present to an extreme degree. Sometimes parents observe in a child the beginnings of patterns described above, but they do not attach any significance to them and therefore take no action. The purpose of the following sections is to alert parents to early indicators of antisocial behavior so that remediation can be attempted *before* the patterns intensify, expand, and become well-entrenched.

When the national television news program ''60 Minutes'' presented the results of the research-treatment study of criminals that Dr. Samuel Yochelson and I had conducted, viewers wrote in and urged that instead of expending so much effort and time helping adult criminals change, resources should be directed toward prevention.[3] In theory, virtually no one could be opposed to prevention. However, society's customary stance toward delinquent behavior is not to prevent it, but to react *after* a youngster has already been arrested. Frequently objection is made to undertaking preventive measures because of the fear of ''false positives'' or wrongly identifying a child as ''predelinquent.'' You may wonder how I can be certain that the behavior discussed, if not corrected, will lead to the commission of crimes. My reply is to suggest that irresponsible and destructive patterns at *any* point in a child's life should be addressed.

In 1980, a review was published of ten delinquency prevention studies that were considered models in terms of their design.[4] The prevention efforts were ''deemed ineffective [in that] treatment produced no better results than an absence of treatment.'' Although the authors of the review concluded that little is known about preventing delinquency, they voiced doubts about whether further studies along such lines should even be undertaken. One obstacle they cited in conducting such studies is that it is ''not altogether clear which acts are worthy of the delinquent label." A second warning claimed that it may be "prejudicial and potentially harmful to those youths who will not acquire records to become targets for 'prevention.' " (Here again is the issue of "false positives.") It was further asserted that it might not be feasible even to conduct future delinquency prevention experiments because of "the extension of legal safeguards to children and greater insistence upon full disclosure to experimental subjects."

After decrying the futility and perhaps danger of trying to identify future delinquents, some social scientists are beginning to regard this as a desirable and feasible endeavor. In 1983, a conference was held in Vermont that focused on early identification and intervention.[5] Although there still was an emphasis on identifying environmental factors that appear to place children at risk, several participants indicated that attention needs to be directed to the personality of the individual child. Professor of child development Emmy Werner stated that, in her long-term study conducted in Hawaii, "children with 'difficult temperaments' . . . had a greater chance of developing delinquent behavior than children who were perceived as rewarding by their caretakers." George Spivack and Norma Cianci suggested that a desirable line of research "is to further articulate the nature of the cognitive and behavioral characteristics of such children and to trace their precursors during early developmental years." Carl Jesness raised the question "How early in life does the child as an individual personality become in part responsible for the events that occur?" With respect to possibly mislabeling a child as a potential delinquent, Dr. Jesness conjectured that if one carefully looked into this matter, there might emerge "considerable reassurance to the effect that the so-called false-positives are not very false at all."

My response to the concern about which acts are "worthy of the delinquent label" is to take the matter out of the realm of labels and laws altogether. Because laws change, the act that is considered a crime today may not be considered one tomorrow. But human nature does not change, and there are moral values that are universal.

For fifteen years, psychologist Lawrence Kohlberg studied moral judgment and character in children.[6] He identified six stages of moral development that are not exclusive to a particular culture, but have a universal nature. In the most primitive of these stages, the badness or goodness of an act is determined by what happens to the perpetrator of the act. The orientation in that stage is in terms of obedience and punishment. The most advanced stage, on the other hand, reflects the individual's developing universal ethical principles.

Some youngsters and adults would act immorally and injure others, no matter what society they lived in. I believe it is desirable to recognize who these children are before their initial involvement in whatever society designates as "delinquent" acts. There can be little doubt that it is possible to identify antisocial patterns early. Research bears this out. For example, a group of psychologists studied aggressive behavior in children over a twenty-year period.[7] They concluded, "Aggression at age eight is the best predictor of aggression at age nineteen, irrespective of IQ, social class, or parents' aggressiveness." In that study, children who were rated as aggressive by their third-grade peers were still evaluated as such when they were in high school.

I believe that not only is delinquency prevention possible, but that it is critically important. And to engage in worthwhile preventive efforts, we must not shrink from the task of early identification. As Canadian psychologist Denis Stott observed, "No preventive measures are possible unless we are able to identify the delinquency-prone."[8]

PART II

THE ANTISOCIAL YOUNGSTER: IDENTIFYING FEATURES

3.

"LIFE IS A ONE-WAY STREET—MY WAY"

Mrs. Simmons asked her fourteen-year-old daughter Linda to wash a few dishes that had accumulated in the sink—a routine request by a mother to a daughter. Linda muttered in a nasty tone that she'd do it later. A few hours before this request had been made, she had slipped home after staying out all night without permission. Placed on restriction, she was forbidden to use the phone, listen to the radio, or watch television. When Linda responded as she did about doing the dishes, something snapped inside her mother. After months of walking on eggshells, Mrs. Simmons was sick of fearing that any time she asked her daughter to do anything, she would be met with defiance and subjected to a barrage of curses and threats. She raced into Linda's bedroom, grabbed some of her jewelry, and declared she would return it only after Linda did what she had been told. Mrs. Simmons does not remember who grabbed whom, but before she knew it, she was involved in physical combat with her own daughter, and Linda was banging her mother's head against a wall. Eventually, overcome by exhaustion, the two released their holds on each other. Months later, when Linda's mother was telling me about this episode, she confessed that she "knew better" than to take on her daughter physically, but Linda had tyrannized her for so long that she was determined that this time her daughter was not going to prevail. The next day Mrs. Simmons filed assault charges against her. A hearing was held in juvenile court, and the girl was ordered into a detention facility.

This terrible ordeal occurred after years during which Linda's mother felt increasingly powerless to cope with her daughter's misbehavior. And it was not the first time that Linda had tried to physically harm her mother. It seemed that for as long as Mrs. Simmons could remember, Linda had expected everything to be on her terms both at home and at school. At school, she had vandalized property, verbally abused teachers, and recognized no obligation to anyone. If Linda liked a teacher or a subject, she occasionally consented to do the work. If not, she made no pretense of interest and refused to do what was expected. The friends she chose were similar to herself. Three of her four close friends had juvenile arrest records, and even with them she had had numerous fallings-out. Linda was truly a law unto herself. It seemed to her mother that she had always been an uncommunicative and angry child. Linda's view of the world was completely uncompromising: She was always right! When she was accused of wrongdoing, she'd complain about others creating problems. Almost never did she accept responsibility for her own actions.

Thinking *only* about oneself is a hallmark of antisocial behavior. But there are people extremely absorbed with themselves who are not antisocial. Furthermore, to varying degrees, we are *all* self-centered: we seek to fulfill certain needs and advance our self-interest. An infant sees the world only as an extension of himself. Incapable of helping himself, a baby is totally dependent on others to fulfill his most basic biological needs. Eventually, the child recognizes that a world exists outside himself, and learns that it is necessary to wait for some needs to be satisfied. The process of socialization requires that a human being accept the fact that other people will not cater to his every wish, that they are individuals in their own right with needs and feelings quite apart from anything having to do with him.

Like any other child, the youngster who becomes antisocial grows physically less dependent on others and able to do things for himself. But the similarity stops there. The antisocial child rejects the efforts of those who try to help him become a responsible, caring human being. Even as an adult, he continues to expect the world to revolve around him. Whether a person will maintain the attitude that life is a one-way street cannot be predicted in infancy. But there does emerge in early childhood a distinguishable difference between the self-centeredness of that age and the selfishness of the child who becomes antisocial.

As the infant becomes a toddler, he plays alongside others (''parallel play'') but not really *with* others. The toddler knows little about compromise and continues to impose his demands on others. Psychologists refer to the two-year-old in terms such as ''the Little King''[1] and ''the insatiable 'I' ''[2] to describe a human being who still expects the world to respond to his beckoning, even anticipate his needs. The toddler is this way because he lacks experience in the social world. He approaches life in a trial-and-error fashion. But, more important, as he learns about that world, he *modifies* his behavior.

The antisocial youngster, however, *continues* to be demanding and insists on having things his way. He remains indifferent to the desires and needs of adults or other boys and girls. In a game, the antisocial youngster strives to control others in either a coercive or deceptive manner. Defeating others at all costs becomes his objective. He epitomizes the poor sport. If others refuse to play by his rules, his response is either to quit or to make their lives miserable. As early as age four, this child's behavior may already be highly disturbing to his parents, other caretakers, playmates, and neighbors. Of course, many boys and girls go through periods of such behavior, but over time it visibly diminishes. The antisocial youngster *remains* determined to outmaneuver and overcome his peers rather than play with them in a cooperative manner.

Children remain somewhat self-centered even as their social world expands. Child psychologist Arnold Gesell, whose writings of more than forty years ago are still quoted, describes the six-year-old as ''the center of his own universe [who is] most secure when he is in control of a situation.''[3] In most cases, it is the young child's quest for his parents' approval that induces him to consider other people's needs and feelings. Gradually, the youngster learns that by taking other people's needs into account he more successfully satisfies his own desire for acceptance and love. And so what pleases, disappoints, or disturbs others becomes of increasing significance to him. Simultaneously, he comes to see people as individuals distinct from himself with their own personalities.

Jean Piaget's work offers important insights into the moral development of the child.[4] In describing how a child over time will involve himself in a game of marbles, the Swiss psychologist identified four stages. The youngest child simply handles the marbles. He is involved in individual play, with no awareness of or regard for collective rules. Between the ages of two and five, he is conscious of the fact that rules exist, but continues to play by himself more than he plays with others. Around the age of seven, he begins to cooperate with others, but ideas about rules remain vague. Finally, between eleven and twelve, ''not only is every detail of procedure in the game fixed, but the actual code of rules to be observed is known to the whole society.''

The antisocial youngster follows a very different course and pays little attention to the ''code of rules.'' He shows little concern about anything except what he wants at the moment. Pleasing other people is never high on the list of what is important to him. The search for parental approval is a powerful inducement to become less self-centered for most boys and girls. Not so with the youngster who is antisocial. To recall Linda's case, from early childhood, she continued to pursue her objectives with little thought for pleasing anyone except herself. At times, she did what her mother requested, but usually with great reluctance. Even as a seven-year-old, she tried to exact a price. The prevailing attitude was ''Now that I've done what you wanted, I want . . .'' When her mother took her to task about her lack of cooperation, Linda would berate her for not appreciating what little she had done. Basically, Linda cared little about what her mother thought. She hardly saw her parent as a person at all. Mrs. Simmons represented a tool for Linda to use to get what she wanted, or she was seen as posing a barrier that Linda would plot to overcome.

It is essential not to confuse the age-appropriate egocentric behavior of young children with the selfishness that becomes an enduring character trait. Psychologist Joseph Church points out that the young child actually is not selfish because he does not yet have self-awareness.[5] A truly selfish person is one who has had experience with life and still chooses to remain focused on himself to the exclusion of other people. The antisocial youngster not only remains focused on himself, but shamelessly uses others to achieve his own ends as well.

Gesell's ''bossy, one-sided, dictatorial'' six-year-old does not remain that way; in the majority of cases, he evolves into the ten-year-old who manifests ''fineness of character, graces of deportment, and perceptiveness of interpersonal relationships.'' At ten, however, the antisocial child may show none of these positive qualities. Instead, he may be secretive, ill-mannered, and manifest an alarming insensitivity to others. But the picture is not always so clear-cut. By age ten, he may not yet have revealed himself for what he is. This child may appear charming, polite, and responsive to the requests of others. Although he appears to care about what people think of him, an ulterior motive may be operative. His good behavior may represent only token compliance or constitute a cynical maneuver to ingratiate himself so that he can take advantage.

A clue that this is happening is that he constantly tries to wrest concessions from others for doing merely what is expected of most children. Rather than genuinely caring about others' approval, his interest is mainly in what he can get from them. Such a youngster may deliberately put up a front. An unexpected and welcome enthusiasm for schoolwork may distract parental attention from what he is doing outside school. He solicits the approval of parents and teachers only because he knows that then they are likely to be off guard, giving him more leeway to do what he wants on the side. Confided one twelve-year-old to me, ''Those kids who act up in class are dumb. I do my work. Then no one really watches what I do outside.''

One might contend that even a responsible youngster

with the sunniest of dispositions is likely to turn into a monster as he enters adolescence. Isn't viewing life as a one-way street a hallmark of being a teenager rather than confirmation that one has an antisocial kid on his hands?

In a monograph titled *Normal Adolescence,* a group of psychiatrists cited as a characteristic of early adolescence "intense narcissism, with a strong preoccupation with one's own body and self."[6] Adolescents do become self-absorbed as they cope with physical changes, strive for social acceptance, and become less dependent on their parents. As they seek autonomy and struggle to develop a more solid sense of who they are, some experiment with behavior that adults consider outrageous or that may be illegal. They may drive too fast, cut a class, overestimate their alcohol tolerance, squander money, and in other ways exercise poor judgment. However, such behavior is episodic and eventually given up, for teenagers learn from the consequences to modify their behavior. But there is far more to adolescence than the much-talked-about storminess. Although at times moody, demanding, and inconsiderate, teenagers as a group are concerned with fairness, they often are amazingly sensitive to others' feelings, they manifest a streak of idealism, they ponder life's purpose, and they are immersed in accomplishing something worthwhile at school, in sports, or in social and community organizations. Despite intense disagreements with adults, adolescents generally accept their guidance and live within the limits that are imposed. In contrast to the basically responsible adolescent is fifteen-year-old Alan, typical of antisocial adolescents who are reluctantly brought to me by frustrated, often desperate parents.

When Alan was in fifth grade, he regarded his parents and teachers as the enemy. He turned virtually any request into an opportunity for battle. He would demand a reason for anything asked of him and then either ignore the response or ridicule it. The smallest thing could become an issue impelling Alan to dig in his heels and argue—taking out the trash, putting away clothes, doing homework. When taken to task for neglecting a chore or assignment, Alan would attack the request as unreasonable to begin with or insist that he had more important things to do. By arguing, he often wore others down so that eventually they gave up and abandoned their requests.

As he entered high school, Alan was completely unmanageable. He refused to get up on time to go to school, even when his parents made sure his alarm was set. One day, when he again arose late, his frustrated father began yelling at him. Alan told me, ''I'd have liked to knock the shit out of him; I hope he has a heart attack.'' Whenever his mother asked him to do a chore or small favor, he'd refuse, and a quarrel would ensue. With some pride, Alan said to me, ''I give her shit; I yell back, and it shuts her up.'' He asserted that only what *he* wanted mattered. For example, he said, ''As far as going out at night, I'll continue to do it.'' About going to the beach, his stance was ''If they say no, I'll go anyway.'' His mother told me, ''Everybody's scared to death; he used to beat his brother into the ground.'' A school report stated that Alan was ''rebellious, impolite, and makes it a point to talk back and draw attention to himself.'' He attended class if he felt like it. When he went to gym, he refused to participate. No matter what the person or situation, Alan emphasized that it was others who must change, not he: "I ain't gonna change for nobody."

This boy came from a middle-class home in which he was raised by both parents. He had a younger brother who was his diametric opposite—honest and dependable. The two boys had the same parents, were raised in the same home, and had attended the same schools. Alan and his brother had been presented with essentially the same expectations and requirements. But Alan pursued only what he considered exciting at the moment. Disappearing from the neighborhood, lying, acting up in school, and fighting were daily occurrences. His depressed and exhausted mother told me, "I've put more energy into *this* child. I couldn't even tell you when my other boy began to walk."

As far back as either parent could recall, Alan had always been self-centered. Rarely had he acknowledged that what anyone else wanted had any legitimacy. Alan's younger brother had been temperamental at times, but his parents saw in him an innate goodness and a sensitivity to other people that Alan did not show.

Seeing life almost exclusively as a one-way street is a hallmark of antisocial thinking. At this point in our knowledge, we cannot predict with certainty whether a particular two-year-old will grow out of being self-centered and de-

manding. In most boys and girls, childlike egocentric thinking does give way to an awareness of and sensitivity toward
others. But the child who is becoming antisocial, instead of
becoming more sensitive to others, *persists* in acting as
though other people exist only to gratify his needs. That
child doesn't care whom he exploits or injures in the process.

4.

DISREGARD OF INJURY TO OTHERS

When I was in the fifth grade, my parents picked me up one day after a school activity and offered to drive one of my classmates home. As we approached her house, Mary asked to be dropped off at the corner and said she would walk to her home nearby. My father would not hear of it because it was dark and he wanted to be sure she arrived home safely. Mary seemed uncomfortable, but dutifully indicated where my father should stop the car. As I curiously looked around, I didn't see a place where anyone could live, and I said to Mary, "You couldn't live here. There's nothing but stores." Pointing to an upper story over a small grocery store, Mary nervously said that this was home, and scurried out of the car. Although somewhat taken aback by my comment, my parents quietly explained to me that many people do live above stores; they pointed out that probably Mary had not wanted to be dropped off at home because she was embarrassed over the fact that she did not live in a single-family house as most of her classmates did. We talked about sensitivity to others' feelings. My father did not have to tell me never to do anything like that again. I was mortified because I had hurt Mary's feelings. After thirty-seven years, I still cringe when I recall this incident. It is hard to believe that I had been so insensitive. I knew that not everyone lived in a house, that some people lived in apartments. But to me a store was a store, and I did not even imagine that people could live in apartments above stores.

Most of us begin to acquire sensitivity to other people's reactions after being hurt ourselves. The process starts early. The toddler grabs a toy from another kid. The same thing happens to him, and he cries. Eventually, he makes the connection between how he feels and how others feel. I remember another incident that had a profound effect on me. I was four years old and was having a birthday party. Kids came to the door, entered the house, and handed presents to me. Pat, a favorite neighborhood playmate, trudged up the walk to the door. As I let her in, I noticed that something was missing. "Where's my gift?" I asked. Pat stammered that she had left it at home. She turned and raced home in tears. Overhearing what I had said, my mother told me in no uncertain terms that people are not required to give gifts. She suggested that it was unkind to put anyone on the spot by asking for a gift. After all, we did not know why the guest that I had invited had come empty-handed. Perhaps her family couldn't afford a gift, or maybe they hadn't had time to buy one. This was another lesson in personal sensitivity.

It has been observed by experts in child development that children as young as two years old "react empathetically to a hurt child."[1] As a child grows older, he not only experiences empathy for others but also reacts by helping the distressed person. By contrast, the child who becomes antisocial derives a perverse sort of gratification from another's pain. Instead of relieving another person's distress, he may inflict more. Even his sense of humor is satisfied at the expense of others. He may laugh when a child trips and falls, or he may taunt an obviously handicapped child.

Usually, the young child, who is a very concrete thinker, becomes aware of the impact his behavior has upon others after he has directly and immediately experienced the consequences of his own transgressions. The child eventually stops grabbing and shoving because he knows how it feels when he is on the receiving end. Or he may modify his aggressive behavior because he knows that if he persists, he will be punished by someone other than the victim. His parents will take action!

In other words, besides not wanting to be victimized himself, the child seeks approval from others. The desire to please is a powerful deterrent to thoughtlessness. Gradually, the child begins to think *before* he acts. Parents can sometimes observe this process verbalized by a young child who, upon facing a forbidden temptation, says aloud to himself, "No, no," and then restrains himself.

The most powerful deterrent to injuring others is conscience. The capacity to experience guilt is an outgrowth of conscience development. Yet in our society, "guilt" has lately been wrongly condemned as a sickness. Among mental health professionals, guilt has been viewed as inhibiting spontaneity, bottling up free expression, and constricting personal autonomy. Popular psychology has exhorted us to cast off the shackles of guilt so that we can better look out for our own self-interest. We have been urged to "look out for number one"[2] and "win through intimidation."[3] Men and women have flocked to therapists' offices to rid themselves of the torment of guilt.

It is essential to make a distinction here between crippling neurotic guilt and guilt that guides us to goodness in our daily actions. One of my patients was guilt-ridden because she evaluated nearly everything she did by her mother's standards. She even felt a twinge of guilt about the furniture arrangement in her home because she believed her mother would prefer some other arrangement. She lacked confidence in many of her own child-rearing decisions because she felt her mother would disapprove. When her mother came from Texas for her annual visit, my patient put her husband and children on notice to "behave." Although this woman was a bright, talented, and accomplished human being, she was miserable because she filtered so much of her life through what she believed her mother would think. This is a prime example of neurotic guilt, a case in which a person suffered from needless guilt.

At the other end of the spectrum was Hank, a young man who did not experience guilt when he should have. Thoughtlessness, crass insensitivity, and exploitation were endemic to his way of life. Hank borrowed money with no intention of repaying it. He was extremely possessive and demanding of his wife's attention and devotion, but he offered little affection or support in return. Instead, he frequently stayed out all night drinking and on the prowl for women with whom he could have extramarital sex. When Hank's wife wanted to know where he had been, he became enraged and threatening. At work, he was also insensitive to other people. His coworkers could never count on him to be there and see a job through. He felt no compunction about stealing from the job site. This man *needed* to experience guilt in order to spare others further injury.

Clergymen and pastoral counselors have long emphasized the goodness of guilt.[4] If we injure other people, we should feel guilty. Besides feeling guilty after we have hurt someone, pangs of conscience should hold us in check when we even *think* of doing something that would harm another. The woman referred to above experienced guilt before, during, and after much of what she did when, in fact, she had done nothing harmful. The man who was a philanderer and dishonest worker was capable of experiencing guilt. But instead he had the capacity, common to criminals, simply to shut off conscience long enough to do whatever was expedient or exciting at the moment. Although he had a conscience, it did not serve as an effective deterrent to injuring others.

We all have times during which our base impulses seem to take over. As hard as we may try to treat others as we would like to be treated, we have lapses and are insensitive or rude. When we recognize that we have hurt someone, we are bothered. If possible, we make amends. We also learn from the experience and refrain from repeating the offensive behavior. Conscience is our monitor.

The youngster who becomes antisocial has only a primitive concept of injury. He thinks of it almost exclusively in physical terms. A person is injured if he is left lying in a pool of blood; otherwise, he isn't. A car thief whom I interviewed in a detention center commented, ''The people who I took the car from ought to thank me because I brought it back in better condition than I got it.'' This could be dismissed simply as a calculated and self-serving statement, an attempt by the offender to portray himself in a favorable way. However, it also reveals an important underlying thought process—failure to consider injury to others, whether it is physical or psychological. This youth had not even a glimmer of the ripple effect his crime had had upon his victims. When I pressed him on the matter, the boy said that he surmised that the car's owner was probably ''mad.'' That was the only consequence that he could think of. I pointed out that when a person has a car stolen, the impact is far greater than a person's being angry because he is without his automobile. The owner must devote time to reporting the matter to the police and to his insurance company. This can entail hours of telephoning, answering questions, and filling out forms. Invariably, the victim has to inconvenience others in order to go to work, buy necessities, and accomplish numerous other daily tasks. After the car has been stolen, the fear lingers that the thief may return to steal something else and harm someone in the process. There are indirect victims, such as those in the neighborhood who become apprehensive about the security of their homes and property and their personal safety. Even after the owner gets his car back, the impact is not over. For a person who has been the victim of a crime, the terrifying feeling of being invaded remains, and life is never the same again.

The perpetrator of the auto theft did not consider himself to have victimized anyone. In fact, he thought that *he* was the victim, because he was incarcerated! The person who is antisocial does not regard his victim as a thinking, feeling human being. The victim is simply an object that impedes or facilitates the offender's doing whatever he wants.

Even in day-to-day interactions that do not in any way involve an arrestable act, the antisocial youngster does not put himself in the place of others. As I indicated earlier, this type of youngster perceives himself as the hub of the wheel, never as one of the spokes. He makes a practice of scrutinizing other people to determine where they might be vulnerable; then he strikes. What he does to others matters little, so long as he attains his objective.

The antisocial youngster is a master at taking people in and then causing them to suffer, especially the members of his own family. As I was talking with the mother of ten-year-old Ken, she said with a sign of relief, "He's been good for a week; I'm feeling hopeful." Shortly thereafter, Ken embarked upon a rampage of stealing, misbehaving in school, and lying to his parents. "I get in trouble," he said, "after I've been especially good." His distraught mother said to me, "It's like an alien living inside him." And yet when Ken was asked how he felt about his parents, he unequivocally declared that he loved his mom and dad. But the terms this ten-year-old boy used said a lot. "They do lots of things for me," he commented and then went on to point out that they gave him toys, took him places with his friends, and permitted him to "buy the stuff I want." Ken described his relationship with his parents solely in terms of the specific things that they gave him. So far as he was concerned, the basis of the relationship was for him to extract as many favors and material possessions from them as he could. He didn't have the slightest recognition of obligations to his family. Rarely did he experience guilt at the turmoil and anguish he caused at home.

In most instances, the antisocial youngster doesn't consider whether or not he is harming anyone. All that matters to him is his immediate objective. Enraged at his mother for grounding him, Tony, fourteen years old, ran away. During the three hours that he was unaccounted for, his parents were frantic. When we discussed the episode later, Tony absolutely refused to focus on how upset his parents were. He declared that he never would have run away or, for that matter, done many other things (including stealing and lying) that his parents objected to if he had been living a "happy life." When I asked him what he meant by a "happy life," he replied, "To not get grounded, for them to stop yelling at me." He continued to denounce his parents, and only after I pressed the issue did he acknowledge that he knew it was wrong for him to steal from his sisters and to lie. But for Tony it was wrong to do these things only because he got into trouble, not because there was anything inherently wrong in lying or stealing. Tony contended that if his parents would give him what he wanted, he would have no need to steal.

I am making three points in discussing Tony. One is that the antisocial youngster knows right from wrong. In his mind, however, he can cloak wrongdoing in righteousness because it is what he wants to do at the time. Because *he* wants to do it, it is right; if someone else does the same thing, then it is wrong. The second point is that, after the fact, the antisocial youngster still does not think about the harm he has done. He is concerned about saving his own skin. He finds the best defense is to go on the offensive and blame others. Tony stole because his parents would not give him all that he wanted; he ran away because they grounded him. Third, the antisocial youngster can thoroughly confuse others and sometimes gain sympathy by emphasizing how good his intentions were. He expects that focusing on his good intentions will obscure or at least mitigate the harmfulness of whatever he did.

The matter of intention is critically important. All of us have hurt someone despite the best of intentions. But we recognized that our good intentions did not make up for or eradicate the damage. Consequently, we felt guilty long after the incident and took pains not to repeat our error. The antisocial youngster, on the other hand, even if he intends no harm, invariably injures not only his immediate victim but also the people who care about him the most.

Consider the following situation. Denise gets into a fierce argument with a classmate who she suspects is trying to steal her boyfriend. The classmate hurls a string of names at her, and the war of words escalates into a hair-pulling, scratching free-for-all. The classmate stumbles, strikes her head on the corner of a desk, and is rushed to the hospital with a gaping wound. The principal suspends Denise and summons her parents to school. Denise claims that she did not intend to hurt her classmate. In fact, she declares that the girl was a good friend. Defensively, she says, "What was I supposed to do, let her steal my boyfriend and call me a bunch of names in front of my friends?'' Emphatically, she declares, ''I didn't mean to hurt her. She threw the first punch. Was I supposed to stand there and take it?'' Immediately, the fight becomes someone else's fault, and Denise becomes the aggrieved party. Her parents are beside themselves and don't know what to do. They both work, and they know that if no one is home to watch Denise, she will roam the streets during the period of suspension. But they are worried about a lot more than the inconvenience of having their daughter at home unattended. Denise's mother had been physically ill from the stress of coping with a daughter who had become incorrigible. Denise claimed that she loved her mother and never had the slightest intention of hurting her. And yet her mother was her chief victim on a regular basis.

A more vivid example of this often misleading issue of intention occurred in the aftermath of a liquor store shooting. The perpetrator claimed that he had no intention of hurting anyone. With indignation in his voice, he noted that during the holdup, the store owner made a sudden move. Explained the offender, ''I thought he was going for a gun; I had to protect myself.'' Blaming the victim is what the antisocial person resorts to as he asserts the purity of his own intentions. Said one boy, ''I wasn't going to hurt the guy. I needed some money. If he had just handed over his wallet, I wouldn't have laid a finger on him.''

Sexual activity is part of the antisocial person's pursuit of conquests and ego buildups. As in the other areas of life, he gives little thought to whom he might hurt in the process. Children are sexually curious from an early age. They may attempt to satisfy that curiosity by undressing with other kids, playing doctor, sneaking a look at sexually explicit magazines, and so forth. Most offenders whom I have interviewed became absorbed with sexual matters very early. Their sexual activities took many different forms and went well beyond typical childhood sex play. The sexual behavior of the antisocial child has a driven quality to it—it is one of many areas of life in which he seeks excitement by doing whatever is forbidden. In other words, these youngsters not only engage in forbidden sexual activities such as peeping, molesting other children, and attempting intercourse, but they also are involved in fighting, lying, stealing, and vandalism.

As they grow older, antisocial youths become irresponsible in their sexual lives, resulting in injury to others of which they are totally unaware. The antisocial individual treats his partner like a piece of tissue paper, to be used and discarded. Innocent people are misled, attacked, and in other ways victimized by him. Frequently, one irresponsible partner finds another irresponsible partner available for a consenting sexual experience. The consequences include disease, unwanted babies, miscarriages, and abortions. Again, there is no intention of injuring anyone.

In summary, what a responsible child is learning by age nine or ten, the antisocial youngster rejects. The responsible child is developing interpersonal sensitivity, so he thinks about the impact of his behavior on others. With experience, his empathy for others grows, and he begins to feel what they feel. By age five, most children have developed an operational conscience. By age nine, they have what Gesell termed a "highly developed ethical sense."[5] The responsible child wants to avoid hurting others not only because he will get punished, but also because he does not want to suffer pangs of guilt. His conscience functions not only to bedevil him after he has done something thoughtless, but also operates to banish malicious thoughts even as they occur in his mind.

"Thou shalt love thy neighbor as thyself" (in the Old Testament book of Leviticus) and the Golden Rule (in the Gospel According to St. Matthew) of "Do unto others as you would have them do unto you" capture a nearly universal quality of how men are enjoined to treat one another. Child psychoanalyst Selma Fraiberg stated, "The capacity to put oneself in the place of another living creature . . . is the indispensable quality in the morality of man."[6] The antisocial person lacks that quality. He rejects the teachings of those who try to help him become a sensitive, empathic human being. He does not develop a concept of injury to others or a fully operational conscience because these are opposed to the high-voltage excitement that he relentlessly pursues throughout his life.

5.

UNREALISTIC EXPECTATIONS AND PRETENSIONS

"I know I'm not perfect, but I don't know what to change to be any better." This was fifteen-year-old Ed's response when I asked him if there was anything about himself that he disliked or wished were different. Talking to Ed, one's first impression might be that this boy "has it all," for he makes an extremely favorable initial impression. Tall, slender, with styled brown hair, and dressed in off-white slacks with a cream-color-and-brown sweater, Ed appears to have stepped out of a fashion magazine. He looks you directly in the eye and responds in a voice that is calm, well-modulated, and seems to say, "I'm in control; I know what I'm about." As I chat with Ed about his future plans, he asserts, "I think I could be a good lawyer." I understand how he can say this. He is intelligent, personable, tactful, and knows how to get a point across. After we've talked a while, Ed says to me in a most sincere manner, "I'm wondering why I'm sitting here; I'd rather be somewhere else." If I hadn't talked with Ed's mother previously, I'd be asking myself the same thing about this seemingly well-put-together kid. However, I know that things are not the way they seem. Mrs. Laurel has related incidents about her son that are totally at odds with the image that he is projecting.

Quick to point out Ed's positive characteristics, Mrs. Laurel had stressed that he is intelligent and a real charmer. But clearly she had not come to consult me in order to enumerate Ed's strengths. She said that there is an Ed whom few people know. Although teachers and guidance counselors had told Mrs. Laurel for years how bright her son was, they had also informed her that he was not living up to his potential. As a high school sophomore, Ed was barely hanging onto a C − average. The immediate problem, however, was not Ed's poor grades, but rather his commission of a serious crime. Without a driver's license, he had taken his mother's car, driven to another state, and then, upon returning, had had an accident, incurring damages of a thousand dollars. Fortunately, neither he nor anyone else was injured. Mrs. Laurel said that she had been concerned about Ed before this incident, for he had committed other thefts and vandalized neighborhood property. These crimes had occurred sporadically over a period of several years, and she had hoped that he had outgrown the behavior. Now she suspected that his destructiveness and failure to achieve in school were related to an underlying attitude that worried her far more than the damage to her car.

Mrs. Laurel said that she thought Ed sometimes was not facing up to reality. She was deeply disturbed by his assumption that whatever he wanted was as good as his. He'd already selected the prestigious college he wished to attend, but he refused to study in order to achieve grades high enough even to be considered by that school. Ed would confidently predict that he'd do well on a test and claim he didn't need to study. Upon finding out that he had done poorly, he'd predictably blame the teacher for giving an "unfair" test. This was indicative of Ed's pattern—thinking something made it so.

In a report of my evaluation of Ed, I wrote:

> His way of dealing with the world is to try to get the most from people with the least effort, opt for the shortcut, see what he can get away with, and calculate his actions so as not to get caught.

Ed had *not* lost contact with reality. Rather, he chose to dwell in the world of his own pretensions. He expected his mother to sign a permission form so he could obtain his driver's license. Because he did not earn her trust, she did not sign. He expected to have designer clothes and said he would earn the money to pay for them. Upon obtaining a job, his attitude toward keeping it was "It's a pain to go to work; you have to stand up eight hours straight." Consequently he lacked the money to buy the expensive shirts, sweaters, and slacks that he craved. Perhaps one day Ed would be a lawyer, but for the moment he was insisting that he had a right to a lawyer to defend him against the charges that his mother pressed after he stole her car. Not only did he demand that she retain the lawyer, but also that she bear the expense. Ed's cocky sense of his own importance and his assumptions about easy success were not based on realistic expectations, but on his pie-in-the-sky thinking.

A person like Ed, who deals with the world on the basis of his own pretensions, experiences disappointment after disappointment and blow after blow to his self-esteem. This occurs because it is just not realistic for anyone to expect to be successful and achieve recognition without exerting effort. It is also highly unrealistic for an individual to make assumptions that others will function on his terms. The antisocial youngster's pretensions far outstrip his performance. And when the world does not cater to his every whim and confer upon him the rewards that he anticipates, he faults not himself, but other people. His perception is that others are putting him down. Consequently, he may interpret the least little thing that does not go his way as a mortal wound to his self-esteem. His self-confidence is shaken easily and frequently, numerous times a day, because it is a product of brittle pretensions and assumptions, not the result of lasting achievements. Although he may not show it, the antisocial youngster is perpetually angry because he constantly feels let down and diminished by others. The anger seems to metastasize like a cancer, and anyone or anything in his way can become a target for its expression.

In a classic volume on psychological development, Erik Erikson makes the point that for the child, "Prestige [is] gained through mastery."[1] He emphasizes that the youngster "gains real strength only from wholehearted and consistent recognition of real accomplishment." The key words here are "real accomplishment." Many volumes have been written about self-esteem, and many troubled people flock to therapists' offices in order to feel better about themselves. Yet self-esteem is not raised by insight or talk alone, but by what a person *does* with his insights. It works the same way at school or on the job. A teacher can encourage or discourage a student but, in the final analysis, nothing boosts a student's self-image more than actually succeeding at something that has required hard work. For the most part, a person's view of his own worth depends not on his intentions, fantasies, or pretensions, but on what he actually accomplishes.

In the idiosyncratic thinking of the infant, expectation is everything. Freud said that the reality principle is introduced when the infant recognizes that expectation and reality are out of sync and he must wait to have his needs met. As the child develops, adults set goals for him, and he learns to set goals for himself. Through trial and error, he constantly revises his expectations about what he can accomplish. He tests his assumptions about the world. The ingredients for success are essentially the same at every age—concentration, planning, and perseverance. The child learns that success usually does not occur by chance, but results from working hard, benefiting from mistakes, and learning to get along with others.

Picture a situation in which an adult is teaching a young child how to play a simple card game. The adult explains the rules, and the two play an open hand to be sure the youngster understands. The child makes errors, but responds readily to correction. If he finds the game difficult or tedious, he may complain. He may become impatient and irritated by explanations because he wants to get on with it so he can play the game. Of course, the child is intent on winning. Still, he is realistic enough to set that immediate objective aside long enough to learn how to play correctly. And he remains willing to play by the rules. For the anti-social child, however, winning is everything. He expects to be the victor in every situation and, if necessary, bends or changes the rules at his whim.

Keith, a six-year-old patient, was posing formidable discipline problems in his neighborhood and at school. He loved card games. I had a deck and asked him what he would like to play. He suggested a game that I had never heard of and offered to teach it to me. (To this day, I'm not sure he didn't make it up.) As we played, I kept thinking that perhaps I didn't understand the rules. Eventually, I realized that there were no rules or else Keith kept changing them to suit his purposes. At the end of each hand, he would smugly announce that he had won. I suggested that we play tic-tac-toe. Keith demanded that he go first and won. Saying, "Winners go first," he then took the lead. When I won and started to go first, he protested. When I reminded him that he had said, "Winners go first," he became irritated, grabbed the pencil, and demanded to play a different game.

And so it went, no matter what we played: Either Keith played by his own rules or changed the rules when he was not winning. There were times that he knew he would lose, and rather than face that, he quit.

Not all children who insist on winning a game turn out to be antisocial. But a boy like Keith expects to dominate in every situation and is totally unprincipled in regard to how he goes about it. To him, other kids are not perceived as playmates, but as impediments to be overcome. When his expectations of coming out on top are not fulfilled, he takes it as a personal affront. Feeling put down and defeated, he retaliates. He resorts to cheating to get his way. He builds himself up by belittling the competition. As he bosses others around, he may be intimidating and cruel. When his authority is directly challenged, his temper may explode and he will lash out physically. Many children suffer physically and psychologically at the hands of an antisocial child who expects to prevail in every situation.

One might argue that expectations of success are the driving force behind many significant accomplishments. It is not the antisocial individual alone who pushes ahead expecting to dominate the competition; the business executive, the professional athlete, and the aspiring actor do the same. However, these individuals recognize that achieving success requires both great personal effort and the development of a superior product. To the antisocial person, success means becoming number one overnight and taking the most expedient route to get there. The *responsible* executive, athlete, or actor knows that success entails more than shoving the competition aside. One gets ahead not simply because one is more forceful or conniving, but because one has had the tenacity to develop and market a desirable product or has trained and disciplined oneself to cultivate a talent or specific skills.[2] The antisocial person expects to succeed simply because he wills it. His mentality is difficult for the responsible person to grasp. Unless there is effective intervention, the antisocial child will seek only to come out on top and because he will care little about how he does it others will be hurt.

There are those people who are not antisocial, but who still maintain illusions about quick success. These individuals also listen to and believe the stories of people reaching the top overnight. But when their expectations of themselves and others turn out to be unrealistic, they react differently from the antisocial person.

Susan, whom I am treating for depression, is a case in point. To meet her, you would never guess that she has severe, long-standing emotional problems. A handsome woman now in her early forties, her vivaciousness and bubbly good humor mask desperation. For most of her life, Susan expected that she would be swept off her feet by a wealthy business magnate who would marry her, treat her like a princess, and establish her as the owner of a high-fashion boutique that caters to celebrities. Still hanging on to these expectations, Susan had reached her early forties and was working in an office, where she earned enough to rent a small apartment and live in a spartan manner. She had not taken an out-of-town vacation in more than a decade, and her social life was restricted to a series of brief, unsatisfying relationships with men and to sporadic friendships with other women. Clinging tenaciously to her dreams, Susan would do little to improve her situation. She saw no point in getting another job if it wasn't in line with her fantasy. She believed it was beneath her to attend singles functions, where she complained that only losers gathered.

Although she dwelled in the world of her unrealistic expectations, Susan was honest and responsible. Despite her hatred of her job, she outlasted the other employees at the office and was valued because she was totally reliable. A law-abiding citizen, Susan had never received even a traffic ticket. She could not conceive of herself experimenting with drugs. In fact, she did not smoke and rarely drank even a glass of wine. Susan continued to live a responsible, although despondent, life, ever hoping for her prince to appear. She alone was the chief victim of her pretensions.

It is different with the antisocial person. As a consequence of his erroneous thinking patterns, other people suffer. Susan did not act as though she had a claim on people or expected to control them. She lived in her own fantasies and suffered because of it. On the other hand, Ed (whom I described earlier) functioned as though other people existed solely to fulfill his expectations. If he did not get what he wanted, he appropriated it for himself by deception or outright theft. If others stood in his way, he became even more determined to outmaneuver them and achieve his objective by whatever means he deemed necessary.

Because his pretensions are rarely modified by his interactions with the world, the antisocial youngster learns nothing about responsible decision making. In order to make a sound decision, one must find facts and weigh alternatives. If one thinks one knows it all to begin with, there is no need to delay making a decision in order to gather facts. Rarely does the antisocial youngster perceive a reason to develop a sense of priorities. If a responsible ten-year-old wants a bicycle, he may select the one he wants based on something that a friend has that he admires. But he is open to considering alternatives and to looking in stores with his parents in order to make comparisons. If he has to share in paying for the bike, he may learn about comparative shopping in order to find the best buy. This way he obtains training in making sound decisions, and he will apply it in the future.

In contrast, the antisocial youngster demands that his parents buy him the most high-status racing bike, and he lets it be known that he will have no other. He resents the mere suggestion that he wait for a sale, and he rejects out of hand the idea of comparative shopping with his parents. If they impose a condition for purchasing the bicycle, such as his earning money toward it by doing extra chores or improving his school grades, he becomes furious and makes life miserable for the whole family. In his view, he is entitled here and now to the bicycle of his choice. (It is such a person who, as an adult, may tell the police that he stole because he didn't have the money to pay the rent, whereas an investigation reveals that all the while he has been riding around in an expensive new car.) Establishing a set of priorities is unnecessary because, according to his way of thinking, if he wants something, he expects to get it—one way or another.

Because the antisocial youngster is so unrealistic about life, he rides an emotional roller coaster. His assumptions turn out to be gross miscalculations, for the world does not cater to him in the manner that he demands. When society does not accommodate him, he grows depressed and angry. Lashing out at others proves that he is someone to be reckoned with and makes him feel better. Relentlessly, he continues to impose his expectations on the world.

Boredom is endemic to the life of the antisocial youngster. This may appear to be a contradiction, inasmuch as he is constantly taking risks and doing what is forbidden. Yet even the toughest, most daring and delinquent youngster is not engaged in heavy action every moment of the day. Frequently, he is irritable and complains of having nothing to do. When he says he is bored, this is not a reference to that occasional temporary tedium or monotony most of us experience. It means that there is no high-voltage activity for him to engage in at the moment.

It is critical to understand just how different the antisocial youngster's experience of boredom is from that of other children. It is a rare boy or girl who has not complained that he or she had nothing to do. Young children may feel bored until they learn to be resourceful enough to entertain themselves. As the child develops interests both within and outside the home, he complains less. Eventually, children reach a point when their dissatisfaction lies in the opposite direction—namely, there is too much to do and too little time to do it. The antisocial child seems bored with life itself. It is as though he lives in a different world. In a sense he does, because very few of the activities that engage the responsible child interest him.

School is a prime case. If you haven't already, you will notice that many of my examples of attitudes of the antisocial child have to do with school. In fact, you may think that I attach far too much significance to how a child functions in the classroom. It is not academic performance per se that I am stressing. School is the place where children spend six or more hours a day. It is the counterpart of going to the job site later in life. At school, one hopes that youngsters will do more than cram information into their minds. It is a place where they will also learn how to function interdependently, will develop good work habits, and will learn how to solve problems and make decisions. While attending school, the youngster will develop the self-discipline of sticking to a task even though it is frustrating, even disagreeable. Attitudes and performance at school usually are predictors of what is to come.

"There must be some reason to go to school, but I can't think of any," muttered one youngster. To him, the teachers, their requirements, and the subjects themselves all constituted a form of torture. He stopped going to school before finishing the eighth grade. It wasn't that he found the work so difficult. In fact, he said that some of the assignments and tests were easy. To him, the whole atmosphere of school was one of stifling boredom. This was an extreme case, and not every antisocial child leaves school early or finds it so oppressive. But even those who stay in school find little about the experience to be inherently worthwhile. The antisocial child is searching for an excitement that no school could offer, regardless of its curriculum.

In short, the antisocial child does not accept life's obligations, demands, frustrations, and challenges. Unlike his responsible counterpart, the antisocial youngster finds little meaning in academic endeavors, hobbies, and other socially accepted activities. To him, life is hardly worth living if he must be like one of those more conforming kids, whom he derisively refers to as "Goody Two-Shoes." Even when all appears to be going well, the antisocial youngster is dissatisfied. From the perspective of a responsible person, Ed had a good life. Although his father had deserted the family when Ed was very young, his mother had remained devoted to him over the years. Grandparents lived nearby, and the neighborhood was a comfortable upper-middle-class suburban enclave. Ed attended school in a system that was known for excellence. But nothing in this privileged life meant anything to Ed. He craved the sort of excitement that was of little interest to his responsible peers. Ed believed that nothing in their world could compete with skipping school, shoplifting, and smashing windows. His expectations were that life should be a roller coaster of excitement. And he resolved that the ride would never end.

6.

TAKING THE EASY WAY

Statesman Bernard Baruch said, ''The art of living lies less in eliminating our troubles than in growing with them.''[1] In effect, Baruch articulated a major process of growing up. Young children seek immediate exits from difficulties, and when they are stymied in their own efforts, they look to adults to extricate them. A major part of socialization is learning that effort and endurance usually pay greater dividends than resorting to shortcuts. Children learn that taking the easy way out may offer no solution at all; that, in fact, operating out of expediency may compound problems.

Taking a shortcut can be tempting to any of us. But if we have our mind set upon a particular objective, we are willing to endure much that is disagreeable as we labor to achieve it. To the antisocial child, virtually anything that requires a struggle is disagreeable. Because he dwells in the world of his pretensions, he sees no reason to put up with anyone or anything that does not gratify his immediate desires.

We all want what we want when we want it. The differences lie in deciding what precisely we want, and what means we are inclined to use to attain it. Psychologist Bruno Bettelheim describes a child who is playing with building blocks:

> Fascinated by the challenge of building a tower, he gradually learns that even if he doesn't succeed immediately, success can be his if he perseveres. He learns not to give up at the first sign of failure, or at the fifth or tenth, and not to turn in dismay to something less difficult, but to try again and again.[2]

The antisocial youngster does not learn to persevere. When he does not succeed immediately, he quits. He remains ready to resort to virtually any means to fulfill instantly his whim of the moment. His anti-work stance emerges early, sometimes before he enters school.

Perseverance is learned early. Consider then what happens when a child who lacks that quality attends school. His fellow classmates are attentive as the teacher drills vowel and consonant sounds, for they are eager to read. The antisocial child is far more excited by agitating the boy next to him than he is by concentrating on the repetitive drill necessary to master the work. He rejects applying himself to nearly any task that requires effort.

Nine-year-old Jack's response to anything that he found disagreeable was to ignore, deny, circumvent, or destroy it. If he was told he could not have what he wanted, he'd take it anyway. He had an allowance, and was offered opportunities to earn more money by doing additional chores. But Jack would have no part of engaging in tedious tasks at home when it was easier and more exciting to pilfer loose change lying on a dresser or remove coins from his mother's purse. He intimidated his eight-year-old sister into helping him steal money; he threatened to beat her to a pulp if she snitched. Sometimes he'd use the money to buy candy, then peddle the candy at a premium price to friends. Jack also managed to get hold of sexually explicit magazines, which he sold to schoolmates. The money he received from these enterprises was used to buy items such as fireworks, which had been forbidden by his parents.

A highly intelligent boy, Jack nonetheless despised anything academic. His usual grades were Us (unsatisfactory) and Ds. Just to get parents and teachers to stop nagging, he'd occasionally do a little work in class. If he thought he could ease the pressure from home by achieving a good grade on a test, he'd glance over the material or, if circumstances were opportune, sneak a look at another student's answers. When a teacher demanded that he stay after school to make up work, Jack scrawled a note saying that he had a doctor's appointment and signed his mother's name. Of course, this nine-year-old's penmanship was a giveaway, and he was caught.

Jack reacted instantly and often violently to people whom he regarded as impediments or nuisances. Rather than work out a problem with a peer, he preferred to use force. He'd attack most youngsters who insulted him. He bragged to me that he "kicked in the balls" a boy who had teased him by calling him "freckle face." Indicating that now he had changed, Jack told me that he had cornered and terrorized a boy, but did not beat him up because "he looked too scared." Jack had not the slightest inclination to compromise or negotiate. Rather than working to solve a problem, Jack's aim was to wipe it off the face of the earth. If he got into trouble, the only lesson he learned from it was to be more careful and avoid getting caught the next time.

Jack's parents hoped that enrolling him in organized sports would be beneficial. So long as he could be the big hero or leader and impress others, Jack seemed to enjoy the activities—but he loathed attending drills and practices. It was the same old story: That which he liked, he did. Otherwise, "The heck with it." The coach seemed not to mind because Jack was a star player. But his behavior became increasingly intolerable at practices, where he distracted his teammates with dirty jokes, shouting matches, and name calling, and tried to egg on team members to fight with him. Eventually, his attendance was so erratic and his behavior so disruptive that he was told not to return. This is not to say that all youthful athletes are always enthusiastic about attending practice. However, from the moment they try out for the team, they automatically assume they should do whatever they are told in order to condition themselves and excel.

Why one child accepts the work ethic and another does not is open to endless speculation. Attitudes crystallize early. Compare two academically gifted students. In elementary school, one applies himself to classwork, is conscientious about homework, and reads independently. He earns top grades. The other receives similar grades, but his pattern is to do as little as he can get away with. In junior high school, both encounter greater competition and must meet the requirements of five teachers who give quizzes and tests and assign papers and long-term projects. The self-disciplined student who is used to applying himself continues to do well. Rather than back away from new challenges, he strives to meet them. The other student, although still qualifying by his test scores for the "gifted" program, shows an abrupt deterioration in the grades he receives for he manages to do well only so long as little effort is required.

One day, abandoning my usual structured discussion format, I suggested that Jack talk about anything he wanted. I promised not to ask questions about homework, tests, chores, or conflicts with his parents. Discussions with Jack about responsibilities and obligations were always laborious for me and distasteful to him. Because the requirements and needs of others were totally outside Jack's interest, he was irritable and almost nonverbal when such topics were discussed. I felt more like a dentist making an extraction than a psychologist trying to help an individual with problems. Now I had what seemed to be a different boy in front of me. As he animatedly talked about firecrackers and firearms, this morose, sullen child appeared transformed. With vivid detail, Jack described blowing up a dead frog with a BB gun and using firecrackers to decimate dead fish. With keen interest, he had followed reports of the assassination attempt upon President Reagan's life, and he recounted numerous details of the event, noting the exact type of weapon employed. Jack rattled on about riding a roller coaster that turned him upside down, and he talked about the movie *Star Wars,* which he claimed to have seen sixteen times. His brand of humor emerged as he joked about a shark biting a bra off a swimmer. Finally, I was hearing about what excited Jack. For him, life was an unending quest for thrills. About the only thought given to the future was a vague apprehension that his parents might ship him off to boarding school. But he had pretty well convinced himself that this was only an idle threat on their part.

Jack sought the easy way out in nearly every situation. Effort, perseverance, and endurance were almost foreign to him. If he disagreed with someone, he would punch him rather than settle differences amicably. If he wanted something but was denied it, he'd steal it. If he wanted credit for something but didn't want to do the work, he'd copy from another pupil. If his parents pressured him too much, his solution was to lie or run away. We might compare nine-year-old Jack at this point with the typical three-year-old, who, according to psychologist Burton White, is far more inclined to value achievement than simply search for the shortcut or most expedient approach to a problem. White makes these observations of children in their third year:

> [The child] will show an interest in achievement, and pleasure in being praised for that achievement.[3]

It is this shift from working problems out with actions to thinking them through that takes place in late infancy.[4]

The three-year-old who is developing very well can . . . introduce, organize, and carry out complicated activities.[5]

Not one of these descriptions applies to Jack or to other antisocial youngsters. Such children develop along very different lines.

I again wish to emphasize that it's incorrect to conceptualize the behavior of the antisocial person simply in terms of a lack of maturity. Unlike Dr. White's industrious three-year-old, the antisocial youth responds to a totally different set of incentives. The three-year-old craves others' approval and will work to earn it. Eventually, he internalizes many of their values. His self-esteem is boosted whenever he experiences success after a struggle. Even though not one soul may know of his struggles, he feels good about himself! The antisocial youth rejects the idea that he should struggle for anything. In fact, he is contemptuous of the "slaves" and "suckers" who do struggle. One teenager asked why he should work at a "slimy" fast-food restaurant for a minimum wage when he could obtain far more money selling drugs and "work" fewer hours. This attitude is strikingly articulated in a best-selling account of one man's life inside a Mafia family:

At the age of twelve my ambition was to be a gangster. To be a wiseguy. . . . To be a wiseguy was to own the world. I dreamed about being a wiseguy the way other kids dreamed about being doctors or movie stars or firemen or ballplayers. . . . My father was the kind of guy who worked hard his whole life and was never there for the payday. . . . My old man's life wasn't going to be my life. . . . Anyone who stood waiting his turn on the American pay line was beneath contempt. . . . To wiseguys, "working guys" were already dead.[6]

At age twelve, this individual was well on his way to becoming a gangster. He not only had ceased attending school, but he had also dropped out of the entire way of life that a boy his age normally leads.

Dropping out becomes a way of life for the antisocial youngster, and this starts early. First, let's talk about school and the difference between two types of students who perform poorly in school—a handicapped learner and the antisocial youngster. There is a major distinction to be drawn. Some children try to acquire verbal and mathematical skills, but because of developmental or emotional problems, their achievement is not commensurate with their effort. These children are willing to work and endure considerable frustration but simply don't master the skills. The important point is that they are willing to struggle to overcome a handicap and may pay a price in terms of lower self-esteem. Even if they decide to abandon academic pursuits, they undertake other responsible occupations. Some of these students enroll in vocational programs and are successful there. Others may drop out of school but enter the work force and support themselves, acquiring new skills on the job.

The antisocial youngster expects school to serve his purpose. Adult inmates at a midwestern correctional facility were asked to brainstorm responses to the following question: "How might schools be designed to help eliminate delinquency and crime?"[7] Their answers included: "Supervise kids and not teach them, more field trips, stress autonomy, kids teach, kids design own classrooms, let them win at what they do, let kids come when they want, more fun in eating, cut competition, redefine delinquency." Clearly, these inmates had not changed one iota since they were students. Their emphasis was solely on how the school should serve them, without a thought about how they should satisfy the requirements of the school.

The antisocial pupil *chooses* not to apply himself. School simply has nothing that he wants other than an opportunity to socialize. And so he follows one of three patterns. Like the twelve-year-old "wiseguy" mentioned above, he may drop out of school. Or because he does not want adults badgering him about school, he may stay in and get by, doing as little as possible. Another possibility is that he may be bright enough to remain in school and receive high grades, which provide him with a good cover for whatever he wants to do when he's not in school.

What of the antisocial youngsters who appear to be learning disabled? Having a true learning disability can be a seriously handicapping condition. Because so many delinquent youths can't read and write, they are often thought to be learning disabled. There are individuals who mistakenly believe that having such a disability is a cause of criminal behavior. A federal court of appeals in Richmond, Virginia, concluded that a youngster could not be expelled from school for distributing drugs because he was handicapped by a learning disability.[8] The assumption was that the criminal behavior was *caused* by the learning disability.

Let's look at the rationale for suspecting such a causal connection. The thinking is that a learning-disabled child experiences academic failure again and again. His antisocial behavior is considered a reaction to the frustration and anger he experiences. How accurate is this? It is true that children who suffer from learning disabilities are at a disadvantage. However, they react to this disadvantage in very different ways. Some compensate by becoming proficient in other areas of endeavor, such as athletics, the arts, or mechanics. Others persist at trying to become academically successful and work much harder than their classmates. There is no evidence that a learning disability drives people to commit crimes. Reporting on an extensive survey of research studies, the U.S. Department of Justice concluded, "The existence of a causal relationship between learning disabilities and delinquency has not been established; the evidence for a causal link is feeble."[9]

In most of the cases I have evaluated, no genuine learning disability is present. The youthful (or adult) offender is illiterate simply because he did not want to take the time and develop the patience necessary to concentrate on learning. Consider what mastery of many academic subjects entails— attention, concentration, drill, repetition, and sticking with a task that may be difficult. The antisocial youngster frequently refuses to engage in such a tedious pursuit.

His search for shortcuts and eventual dropping out of activities occur in places other than school. Most boys and girls participate in a variety of activities and through trial and error discover where their interests lie. A girl takes piano lessons, but then finds that competing *but neverthe-*

less responsible interests overshadow her desire to play the piano. So she discontinues the lessons in order to do something else. Sometimes youngsters drop out of activities due to frustration, but usually after a sustained effort. A boy takes up tennis, but after six months grows discouraged enough to quit because he still is not hitting the ball and lacks the coordination to progress. The antisocial youngster drops out usually because he does not find it easy to become an overnight star. The responsible child may drop out of an activity after much struggle and disappointment, believing (perhaps mistakenly) that he cannot succeed. In most instances, he gives up less quickly than the antisocial child because he never anticipated achieving success overnight.

When the antisocial youngster takes a shortcut, he entertains not the slightest doubt that he will succeed. Ted told me that he expected to be awarded an athletic scholarship to attend college. He downplayed the fact that as a high school junior he had a D average and a history of suspensions for serious misconduct. As Ted was speaking to me, he was envisioning the glory of playing college varsity football— with no intention of studying for the next day's midterm exams. This was in line with his customary approach: Just by expecting something, he would find that it would come to pass easily. No work was necessary.

Drug use offers yet another shortcut. The prevalent view is that people use illegal drugs to escape their problems, but I have interviewed dozens of individuals for whom things are going well. They have devoted families, remunerative jobs, good health, and plenty of leisure. These people turn to drugs because they do not accept life as it is. They want a far higher voltage to life than living responsibly offers. They are intolerant of the day-to-day frustrations that are a part of most lives. Drugs provide an easy way out in that they obviate the need for one to struggle with life's daily problems.

Growing up poses problems for everyone. The youngster who uses drugs rarely copes constructively with the critical developmental tasks of adolescence. Instead of gaining self-confidence by acquiring an education, developing social skills, forming a value system, and learning to resolve conflicts constructively, the drug user stays in his own world. Fifteen-year-old Jay told me that he knew that some kids get a lot out of life without using drugs, but he could not imagine what. Jay said that when he did not use drugs, life was a "drag." He could not imagine just going to school, doing his work, and living like most other kids, including his brother. Off drugs, Jay felt lonely, insecure, and ill at ease, especially around girls. When he was on drugs, which was most of the time, Jay felt on top of the world. In fact, on drugs Jay would take risks that were unusual even for him. Speeding on a motorcycle while intoxicated, stealing from stores, and having sex with young girls occurred only when he was high. On drugs, Jay felt there was nothing he couldn't do. Drugs were his ultimate shortcut; he did not have to face himself. I stayed in touch with Jay for several years, and found that when he was eighteen, he had no job skills, was thousands of dollars in debt, had served time in a detention center, and had alienated family members who had been supportive of him. Feeling able to lick the world when he used drugs, in reality he lacked the knowledge and social skills of an average fourteen-year-old.

Because the antisocial youngster is perpetually seeking the most expedient way to go through life, he digs himself into one hole after another. Rarely does he heed warnings that seeking the easy way out will result in tragedy. Unfortunately, not until a personal tragedy does occur is he likely even to begin to consider seriously an alternative way of living.

7.

LYING AS A
WAY OF LIFE

Chronic lying is a pervasive behavioral pattern of the anti-social youngster. He lies to conceal wrongdoing or exon-erate himself from blame. But because many responsible children lie on occasion, one could reasonably argue that it is problematic, even dangerous, to conclude that a young boy or girl is antisocial simply because he tells tall tales, exaggerates, or makes up stories. Lying serves different needs at particular points in a child's life, and it is important to recognize what those needs are. It is one thing for a preschooler to try to outdo a playmate by exaggerating the number of birthday gifts he received. It is another for a child to get a thrill out of habitual lying because it is exciting, makes him feel superior to others, and gives him a sense of power.

Preschool children blur the distinction between fantasy and reality. Psychologists Stone and Church point out: "Because the child's world is a mélange of the real and fantastic, he may seem, to adults uninstructed in his ways, to be playing free and easy with the truth."[1] A child who comes to distinguish reality from fantasy may continue to lie because it fulfills current needs. As child psychologist Haim Ginott observed, "Lies tell truths about fears and hopes. They reveal what one would like to be or do."[2] And so a child boasts to a playmate that he is going to get a new bicycle, when in fact one has not been promised. To a friend who has just told him all about an airplane ride, he replies that he has ridden in an airplane ten times, whereas he has never set foot in one. He fibs to his mother by saying that his nursery school teacher told him that he draws the best pictures of anyone in the class. By telling such lies, a child may be striving for what may prove at best to be temporary approval or admiration from the listener. He will learn from experience that, in the long run, misrepresenting himself will usually bring him condemnation and rejection.

Long after children turn four, it is not unusual for them to lie to avoid unpleasant consequences. A child tells his mother that he has no idea who knocked over the vase. He blames his brother for something that he did himself. Silverman and Lustig call such a child an "escaper" in that he is seeking to escape detection.[3] Stating, "Escapers are not serious liars," the psychologists observe that such youngsters are likely to cease lying if "helped to behave more appropriately."

Stone and Church note that because the exaggerations and fantasies of the preschooler "are not a moral issue," they should not be of great concern to parents. Gesell points out that by the age of five and a half, the youngster "usually distinguishes fact from fancy," and by age seven, most children demonstrate "increasing concern over the wrongfulness of lying."[4] Gesell describes the typical nine-year-old as "essentially truthful and honest."

Psychologist Piaget conceives of lying by the child as "an essential part of the child's egocentric thought."[5] He observes that children advance beyond such egocentricity as they grow interested in the results of their own actions. The youngster first thinks of lying as "naughty" when he is aware that he will be punished for doing it. (One can understand the appeal of the children's story of Pinocchio, in which every time the puppet lies, his nose grows longer. To become a real boy, Pinocchio has to develop a conscience.) Finally, according to Piaget, the child evolves to the point that his intelligence "works on moral rules" so that he "feels from within the desire to treat others as he himself would wish to be treated." Thus he comes to regard lying as undesirable, regardless of whether the liar is caught and punished.

Often, lying is not called lying, especially when we speak of adult deception. Instead, we hear of coloring, bending, shading, or stretching the truth. (Sissela Bok wrote an entire book on the "many guises" of deception in contemporary adult life.[6]) In an end-of-the-year cover story, *The Washington Post Magazine* described 1987 as "the year of the Big Lie and the medium lie and the little lie and the teeny-weeny lie."[7] According to a *Washington Post* telephone survey, 507 of 513 respondents owned up to having occasionally told a lie. Distinguishing between the "white lie," which is not intended to harm anyone, and the "serious lie" that conceals wrongdoing, the majority of those polled believed that people infrequently tell the latter type.

When we tell the ostensibly innocuous white lie, the objective usually is to give a momentary lift to or to preserve our self-esteem. We may hope to avoid embarrassment, to escape blame or simply to get our way. We also lie for reasons that we consider to be altruistic. Bad news may be concealed in order to prevent another person's worry and suffering. We may lie because we believe that we are acting in someone else's best interest; for example, we tell a child that he won't be strong if he doesn't eat spinach and reassure him that a medicine doesn't taste bad when we know it is vile. Much can be said about the perceived advantages of lying under specific conditions, but it is important to recognize that for the *responsible* person who tells a lie, lying does not become a way of life. He deals with the world in an essentially truthful manner.

When, during lectures, I have presented a profile of the antisocial person, I am often met with the assertion that to be successful it is necessary to lie. My listeners cite perjury among highly placed government officials, misrepresentation by corporate executives, the living lie of the outwardly clean-cut athlete role model who conceals his drug use, and numerous other examples of people in the limelight who are corrupt. Some have concluded that deception is a frequent, even necessary, business practice in order to defeat the competition. Expressions such as "nice guys finish last" suggest that the person who is trustworthy and honest is at a distinct disadvantage compared with the individual who will sacrifice truthfulness for his own gain. I have flatly disagreed with the assertion that dishonesty is essential to success, for there are people in all walks of life who owe their success to a combination of talent, hard work, and integrity. Without the integrity, the other two ingredients usually do not suffice—at least not for long.

If we acknowledge that we all lie at times, what then distinguishes the antisocial youngster from others who lie? At what point does lying become a matter of real concern? Stone and Church state: "It is only when the child's lying becomes so constant and pervasive that he seems to have lost trust either in his parents or in himself that parents need become seriously concerned."[8] The child who becomes antisocial will have engaged in an expanding and intensifying pattern of lying that takes increasingly sophisticated forms. The two major types of lies are those of commission and omission. The first consists of stories usually concocted on the spur of the moment when the child wants to cover his tracks or to bail himself out of trouble. He makes up a story or excuse that he believes will be plausible enough to help him avoid detection and unpleasant consequences. More often, he lies by omitting facts. He becomes adroit in telling part of the truth while convincing others that they are hearing the total truth. Ten-year-old Bobby tells his mother that he and Jim watched television at Jim's house, which is true. What he omits, in reply to his mother's inquiries, is that the two boys left the house after viewing one program and sneaked through the neighborhood playing "I Spy" by peeping in windows.

On television, stations used to flash a sign that said, "Parents, do you know where your child is?" Most of the parents who have consulted me do endeavor to keep track of their children's whereabouts. They set limits and require their children to inform them where they are going. But unless these mothers and fathers were to function full time as detectives, they could not possibly be aware of all their children's comings and goings.

It has often been said that one reason children turn to crime is that a communications gap exists between themselves and their parents—parents who do not know how to talk to them and do not care about their activities. Such a communications gap does exist, but it is one created by a very secretive child who, if he talked at all about his day, would lie to his parents about where he went, lie about whom he was with, and lie about what he was doing. In fact, such a child rebuffs most attempts by his parents to communicate, and the gap becomes a chasm as the child grows older and ever more secretive. The parents eventually discover that their trust has been misplaced. The child has interpreted their trust in him as a sign of weakness, not as a sign of faith. Time and again, such children exploit and betray parental trust and then angrily berate their parents for not trusting them. They blame their mother or father rather than their own lying or other completely irresponsible behavior, which initially created the breach of trust. Unfortunately, when a counselor is consulted, he, too, is likely to focus on the parents and not grasp that the child's lack of integrity is the salient issue.

Al, nine years old, is one such child. His mother brought him to me because his stealing and then lying about it were increasing by the day. At first Al was pilfering food from the pantry or refrigerator and then claiming that he had not even entered the kitchen. His mother was puzzled about why Al would steal food when all he had to do was to ask for it. She would have given this relatively minor misconduct little thought were it not for similar infractions. Al's younger brothers and sisters would come crying to their mother about toys that were broken through no fault of theirs. Al, however, rarely complained of a broken toy and claimed he knew nothing about his siblings' destroyed possessions. Al's stealing and lying were not limited to home. In his room, his mother discovered candy, toys, and other items that she did not remember buying. Al would tell her a classmate or neighborhood playmate had given him the item in question, when he actually had been stealing from desks, coatrooms, neighbors' yards, and stores. "Scheming" and "manipulative" were among the adjectives that Al's mother applied to her son as she described his denials, excuses, and coverups. The lying seemed to alarm her more than the stealing. She simply could not fathom why a child of hers, who could have nearly anything merely by asking, would act this way. Whenever she questioned her son about any wrongdoing, he had an explanation so plausible that she wanted to believe it. The most alarming and recent episode, which impelled her to seek professional advice, was not a theft, but a dangerous act about which Al blatantly lied. Al terrified little children by shoving them into a swimming pool and then completely denied having been anywhere near the youngsters. Because he had crept up from behind to perpetrate the act and had done it swiftly, he was not immediately caught. Finally, another youngster identified him as the culprit.

Actually, very few people suspected that Al could be the culprit in any offense, for he appeared to be soft-spoken and polite, a model child. He knew this and exploited it whenever he could. On the first day of school, he sized up his mild-mannered, affable teacher as "soft" and predicted to his mother, "Lots of kids will get away with lots of stuff." This was prophetic in that Al stole more than usual from his classmates and even from the teacher.

Al told me that he realized that people should tell the truth, and he made it clear that he knew the difference between the truth and a lie. He confided that there had been times when he resolved "to tell the truth right away, to tell everything that happened." This resolve rarely lasted. Days would pass during which Al appeared to behave well and to be truthful. Desiring to trust her son, his mother would be lulled into thinking that his efforts to reform were genuine. Invariably, every time Al's credibility had been restored by a spate of good behavior, another incident occurred to erode it. His wrongdoing and then lying by either commission or omission persisted, and parental trust reached ever deeper lows.

Like Al's mother, many parents have declared to me that when their child does something wrong, it is the brazen lying, even in the face of incontrovertible evidence, rather than the offense itself that bothers them most. One boy routinely wore clothes from his brother's closet without permission. His parents objected to this "borrowing," but they were even more enraged by the fact that the boy constantly lied about where he found the clothes. Looking his father in the eye, he would come up with such implausible explanations as "The clothes just turned up in my room; I don't have the slightest idea why or how they got there." The whole issue might even have been downplayed were it not for the boy's pilfering small sums of money from his siblings as well. Even when he was told that if he confessed, there would be no punishment, he denied his culpability. Slowly, the parents realized their son had no respect whatsoever for the truth. He derived excitement not only from the offense itself but also from continuing to place the burden on others to "prove" his guilt. Stonewalling had become such a way of life that his family remained continually in the dark about past misconduct and future intentions.

But what confuses most parents whom I have counseled are the lies their children tell that seem to have no purpose. More than one perplexed parent has told me that he or she could not understand why a child would resort to telling a lie when telling the truth would be without risk or even advantageous. The youngster seemed to lie just for the sake of lying, even about the most trivial matters. Because these children lie frequently and almost as automatically as they breathe, parents, mental health professionals, and teachers sometimes regard them as pathological or compulsive liars. Repetitive lying is perceived as an "illness" because it appears the youngster has no control over it.

But by examining this pattern more closely, we find that an explanation for it does exist, one that has nothing to do with compulsion or other mental illness. A teenager says that he rode in a green Ford when it was in fact a red Chevrolet; a boy reports that he had a snack at one fast-food establishment when he really ate at a different one. Only when one examines such lies from the point of view of the liar does the pattern begin to make sense. For the liar, there is power in lying. By lying he keeps others in the dark and thereby believes he has gained the upper hand. He delights in believing that he has pulled the wool over the eyes of others, that no one really knows what he is doing. By lying constantly and in numerous ways, he keeps the world at bay. He revels in the belief that no one really knows him, and this belief enhances his view of himself as special, even unique.

The tactical aspects of lying are often ingenious. The individual keeps others baffled by being vague. "I guess," "In a sense," "Maybe," "Perhaps," and "You could say so" are only a few of the retorts of a youngster intent on secrecy. Occasionally, an antisocial youngster is vague because he truly is unsure, but more often his vagueness is a form of lying. When he says "Perhaps" or "I guess," usually there is no uncertainty. The boy or girl knows what the facts are and who the culprit is, but does not want to make any admissions.

Another tactical approach in lying is to minimize the seriousness of what was done. "Me and my buddies were just messing around," a youth will say. "Messing around" is a euphemism for skipping school and joy-riding around the city. A teenager will say, "I had a little beer," when really, he downed a six-pack. Still another form of lying is to do the opposite and exaggerate for shock effect. (A teenager who drank several cans of beer might brag to a friend that he consumed a case of it.) To elicit strong emotional reactions from others (to "push their buttons," as it is termed in the vernacular) enhances his sense of power.

These tactics are also deployed on occasion by children who are not antisocial. They may understate the seriousness of their wrongdoing or may be vague to avoid being pinned down. But the antisocial child is quite different: He incorporates lying in its many forms into a way of life that conceals his activities. His pattern of lying becomes ever more frequent and sophisticated, but I must stress there is nothing compulsive about it. It is not an illness. That youngster will tell the truth if he or she is convinced that to do so will serve his or her purpose.

When the antisocial child is caught lying, his chief regret is that he was discovered. Rarely does he experience pangs of conscience because he regards lying as morally wrong and injurious to others. If he is pressed to find a lesson in the incident, he'll believe it is that he needs to be more ingenious to avoid getting caught in the future.

The antisocial youngster does not regard himself as a liar, and is likely to express outrage if referred to as such. If asked, he may acknowledge that it is wrong either for him or anyone else to lie. Moreover, he will be indignant, even furious, when he suspects that others have lied to him. At the time he lies, the antisocial youngster has eliminated from his thoughts all consideration of the wrongfulness of what he is doing—he is merely doing what he finds necessary to attain his objective. A lie is a tool for him just as a spade is a tool for a gardener. This attitude is a far cry from that of Gesell's seven-year-old, who shows increasing concern over "the wrongness of lying," or from the child whom Piaget describes as discovering that "truthfulness is necessary to the relations of sympathy and mutual respect."[9]

8.

"IT'S NOT MY FAULT": REFUSING TO BE HELD ACCOUNTABLE

It's common for children and adults alike to blame others as they attempt to wriggle out of admitting a wrongdoing. "He started it" is a response parents and teachers—in fact, anyone who deals with children—hear repeatedly. In a sense, it seems to be part of human nature to blame other people or circumstances in order to divert attention from our own shortcomings. Yet while the responsible person may do this on occasion, he more often will acknowledge his errors, learn from them, and make an effort not to repeat them.

Children and adults who are antisocial seem to have

almost unlimited excuses for their own misconduct. In faulting others, they present themselves as victims and often sound convincing to whoever takes them to task. However, it would be preposterous to conclude that any young child who blames others for his own misbehavior will become antisocial.

The very young child does not have a clear concept of cause and effect when it comes to understanding the impact of his own behavior. He certainly does not have clearly delineated ideas about social relationships. If a toddler slings an object into the air and it strikes a nearby child, it may not be evident to the former that something untoward has happened as a result of *his* actions. Psychologist Gesell points out that a young child's natural inclination is to blame others.[1] A four-year-old may knock something over, turn to anyone in the immediate area, even the cat, and assert, "Now see what you made me do." Gesell says that this kind of blaming, which may include faulting inanimate objects, continues until the age of seven, and even then the child still "may alibi in order to cover up any of his mistakes."

It is at age eight, notes Gesell, that the child is more inclined to assume responsibility for his behavior and suffer the consequences. Even then, there is by no means a complete cessation of the courtroom-type scene in which children, confronted by an adult after a mischievous episode, blame one another. But by age nine, continues Gesell, the child "accepts blame fairly well." He is developing a set of ethical concepts, and is more willing to accept responsibility for what he does.

Nevertheless, as we grow older, we all still occasionally

blame outside circumstances. We play tennis and blame a sudden breeze for a shot going out of bounds. We curse our bad luck for investing in a stock based on a rumor that turns out to be unfounded. We blame congested traffic for our tardiness. Sometimes we are correct; adversity does occur through no fault of our own. If the sudden breeze hadn't sprung up, our shot would have been good. Perhaps there was no way we could have anticipated that at ten in the morning there would be a massive traffic jam. But at times we blame others when we ourselves have been the creators of or contributors to the adversity. If we had conducted careful research or sought out competent advice, rather than purchasing a stock on impulse, we might have avoided a financial loss. If we had allowed extra time in case something went wrong on the highway, then we might have avoided being late. It is often convenient or expedient to blame circumstances rather than shoulder responsibility and attack a problem or even plan ahead to prevent it from occurring.

Deterministic explanations of human behavior have furthered the tendency to blame that which is external to the self. The view that man's behavior is molded principally by the environment is conducive to regarding him as a victim of events beyond his control. In explaining what causes crime, practically every adverse circumstance imaginable has been cited, including poverty, racism, broken homes, child abuse, the glorification of violence in the media, deficient schools, unemployment, adverse influence by peers, and poor role models. While it is true that their environment has an impact on people, individuals differ in how they cope with it. In most cases, they need not be hapless victims of the environment.

Growing up in poverty is one example. A drug dealer whom I interviewed told me that he and his eight siblings were raised in a poor rural area of West Virginia where his alcoholic father eked out a living as a tenant farmer. He said that a person would have to have lived exactly as he did to truly understand how terrible it felt to go to bed hungry, how mortified he was when classmates laughed at him because he wore raggedy clothes, and how incredibly envious he felt of peers who owned things he could only dream about. As a child, he vowed that one day he would surround himself with luxury, which as a seller of narcotics he eventually was able to do. A background investigation conducted by a court official verified his statements about the grinding poverty of his youth. But the court official also learned that none of the offender's eight brothers and sisters had either a criminal record or a history of drug abuse. All were employed at legitimate occupations; some were supporting families. Each of these individuals had been a victim in that, through no fault of his own, he had suffered extreme deprivation. But that deprivation did not ''force'' them into crime.

Of course, sometimes people truly are victims. But even then, as in the case of the drug dealer, individuals choose the way they respond to their victimization. To believe that human behavior is determined by external forces over which we have no control furthers the tendency to blame others rather than look for ways to cope with adversity and to improve ourselves. It slights the fact that sometimes people have the power to make choices to alter circumstances they did not choose.

When very young, the child who later develops pronounced antisocial patterns seems no different from any other youngster in that he blames people because he does not know any better or because he wants to save face. But eventually a more sinister aspect to this habit appears. Rather than having fewer reasons to blame others, he has more, because increasingly he is engaging in conduct that he desires to hide. He knows right from wrong, but in his mind, right is whatever he wants to do at the time. He is well aware that eventually he will be apprehended, but in his own mind it is never *this time*. He has the capacity to shut off the fear of getting caught long enough to do what he wants at the moment. When he miscalculates and is caught, he will automatically blame anyone or anything. It becomes a *way of life* for him to present himself as the victim. As he grows older, he develops an increasingly sophisticated set of tactics to divest himself of responsibility, fool others, and escape consequences.

It's impossible to differentiate between a responsible and an antisocial youth just by looking at a single act. Instead, one has to know the overall mentality that is at work. Two ninth graders, for example, receive Ds on a test and blame the teacher for giving an unfair test. Such a response hardly sounds indicative of a future criminal. But consider the personality patterns of the two outraged boys in question. One had studied hard; the other had not opened a book. In the case of the first student, two possibilities for the reaction exist. Either he failed to master the material, or the test really was unfair. But either way, despite his frustration (and possibly registering a protest about the exam to the teacher), this student vows to study harder the next time. In the second case, the student had no interest in the subject matter to begin with and therefore no intention of learning from the experience in order to improve. Following his customary habit, he diverts attention from his own lack of interest and effort by blaming the teacher.

The antisocial child often is successful at convincing others that whatever the problem, its source lies outside himself. Consider fifteen-year-old Tim, who has made life so miserable at home that his parents reluctantly have decided to send him to boarding school. Furious, Tim refuses to go. He asserts that his parents do not care about him, that their only interest is in getting rid of him. He bitterly accuses them of favoring his sister, of discriminating against his friends just because they dress in an offbeat manner, and of always blaming him when something goes wrong. His list of injustices is unending. Yet his mother and father had agonizingly reached the boarding school decision only after two years of utter misery as Tim skipped classes, refused to do homework, drove their car without permission, stole money from them, came in late at night reeking of alcohol, and refused to attend counseling sessions. Tim's mom and dad knew that they had given him every opportunity to receive help and to change, but they still felt that they had failed as parents. They did not want to send him away. Hoping to find the most suitable school, they consulted a professional placement service. Tim continued to plead for one more chance, begging to stay home and attend the local public school. (Expensive private day schools had been tried, and each time Tim had been asked to leave for serious infractions of rules.) After the parents were interviewed, Tim was interviewed alone by the placement service director. He turned on the charm, telling her he had learned from his mistakes, pleading for a final chance, and promising not to disappoint his parents. He said he wanted to put the past behind him and turn over a new leaf. Tears welled up in his eyes as he complained to the counselor about his parents, especially about their bigoted attitude toward his friends. After listening to and questioning Tim, the counselor was impressed by his apparent sincerity in regard to changing his ways. Tim had been successful in convincing her that his parents' behavior had been more unreasonable than his own and that, indeed, *they* were the cause of his misbehavior. The placement service director decided Tim was simply going through normal adolescent turmoil and that his parents needed to be more tolerant and forgiving. She concluded that Tim should remain at home.

His parents were devastated. They did not know which way to turn. They only knew that their son's *behavior* was far beyond their control, that he had failed to respond positively to anything they did, and that they were out of ideas for the future. Fortunately, the placement director at last saw for herself how quickly Tim appeared to lose control of himself. Bringing the parents and Tim into the same room, she watched a polite, considerate child transformed. Tim became increasingly loud and argumentative, and then turned accusatory and verbally abusive. Observing this heated interaction, the woman reversed herself and concluded that she held little hope that life at home would improve for Tim or his parents and agreed to look for a suitable residential placement. She capitulated to the request, however, principally because she believed the parents were inadequate to the task of nurturing their son.

Tim had convinced a neutral party that he was the victim and his parents the victimizers, whereas the opposite was true. His parents, while being loving and patient, had suffered enormous abuse and begun to believe that the failure was theirs, not his. I supported the decision to send their son to boarding school and assured them that they had left no stone unturned in their efforts to help him.

My point in retelling this story is simple. Like the placement director who was counseling Tim and his family, most people fail to recognize the antisocial child for what he is. This happens not only when such a child is young, but also, as with Tim, when he is an adolescent or even a young adult.

Childhood often is romanticized as a period of treasured innocence. Jean-Jacques Rousseau, the eighteenth-century French philosopher, urged his readers to "hold childhood in reverence." He believed that a young child could do nothing morally wrong because he lacked a concept of right and wrong. Proclaiming "God makes all things good," he believed that children fall into wrongdoing when they are corrupted by external forces. He even went so far as to assert, "Children's lies are entirely the work of their teachers."[2]

It is true that a young child may do something harmful out of innocence. But a tendency exists among some adults to discount the significance of even willful and persistent dishonest or malicious acts by a child, either with the view that the motivation was innocent or that the child will grow out of it. Lies are regarded as childish exaggerations, fights as the results of inevitable squabbles and overreaction, vandalism as pranks, disruptive behavior in school as mischief. Even when the youngster is held accountable and punished, adults often look for explanations in factors that appear to lie outside the child's control. They will not acknowledge that even very young boys and girls may *choose* to lie, fight, and steal. Instead, some adults remain all too ready to accept whatever excuse the child offers just because he is a child. The antisocial youngster counts on this and achieves what he considers victory after victory because he has outsmarted others. He is so ingenious at convincing others that he is the victim that sometimes the real victim of his irresponsibility is ignored.

Perhaps nowhere in the recent past has this tendency become more alarmingly pervasive than in juvenile court. During proceedings that occur behind closed doors to protect the rights of the defendant, there is a tendency to search for explanations that might mitigate the child's responsibility for the crime. During the hearing, the defendant is a very real human being, there in the flesh. The victim is not present. He is reduced to an abstraction, a name, a written police report, or at best a brief written "victim impact statement." Originally, the juvenile court was established to provide services to improve the child's welfare. The thinking was that most children could improve their behavior if offered a wholesome environment, love, and, if necessary, a mild penalty to discourage dis-

obedience. It was believed that children became delinquent through no real fault of their own. The view of the
wayward child as victim was prevalent and to some extent
still is. I don't mean to imply that this remains the thinking in every case or in every court. In fact, I have testi-
fied before juvenile judges who, besides considering
environmental factors, conscientiously delve into the personality of the defendant. Before imposing sentence, they
endeavor to understand how he functions from day to
day. In my view, a consideration of the individual's personality, in addition to the nature of his offense, is absolutely essential. Today's juvenile courts have a great deal
more to cope with than wayward children. Coming into
the courts today are savvy, street-wise antisocial boys and
girls who successfully exploit the still widely held view
that children who commit crimes are victims of circumstance.

The antisocial youngster always knows his explanations
of wrongdoing are just excuses. That is, they are not part of
his thinking before or during an offense. A child will say he
"borrowed" a transistor radio and intended to return it. But
at the time he took it, no such intention existed. He may
claim he threw a punch because he had to defend himself,
when in fact he was the one who mercilessly taunted and
threatened another boy, provoking a fight. The justifications
are articulated only for purposes of accountability. They
have little or nothing to do with why the child committed
the offense.

Blaming others for our own failings is something that we
all do from time to time. But the antisocial child does this

almost automatically any time he is called to account for misconduct. He becomes increasingly resourceful in developing and deploying tactics designed to dupe others and confuse them about where culpability lies. He is so convincing that he often succeeds in minimizing or completely avoiding punishment—and then goes on to victimize others. At his most successful, he truly persuades his listeners that whatever the issue is, he's not at fault.

9.

AN ISLAND UNTO HIMSELF

People relate to one another mainly in terms of experiences that they have in common. Listen to a group of middle-class mothers. Regular themes of their conversations are their marriages, children, finances, careers, and aging parents. They may have differing points of view and approach problems in different ways, but they learn from one another as they work through problems shared by all. Facing life's dilemmas binds us to one another.

The person who is antisocial does not think he has much in common with anyone, at least inwardly. He divorces his life from that of others and believes he has little to learn from them. By diminishing others or through indifference to their problems, he builds himself up. So far as he is concerned, he is uniquely above the day-to-day troubles of most human beings. Listen to statements by an antisocial teenager and a convicted felon, indicating their perception that they have a singular set of attitudes and way of thinking.

> *Fifteen-year-old boy:* I know how all humans think except for me. I think a lot differently from anyone else.

> *Convicted felon:* I've got an attitude about myself that's different from other people. I look down on people—the way they look and act. I'm tougher than them. People look up to me more than them. I'm better looking than them.

Of course, every human being is unique; there are no exact duplicates. But the antisocial person's view of himself suggests that he barely considers himself part of the same species as the ordinary mortal.

And still, after all that I have said in preceding chapters about the development of the antisocial child, it may still be surprising that I now characterize him as a loner. This child is not hiding in a corner. In fact, just the opposite is true. From all outward appearances, it looks as though he is far more sociable than many of his peers. Watch him on the playground, in the classroom, on a street corner, and he will seem to be in the thick of things, not shrinking away from other boys and girls. By the time he is an adolescent, his parents rarely see him, for he is spending most of his time at teenage hangouts.

The appearance of sociability belies the facts. Although he is often with people, this is a child who remains a stranger to them. The antisocial child keeps others at a distance, in part because he is intent on concealing what he is doing. But he also does not reveal himself to others because he believes that there is little benefit in doing so. This youngster lives by his own set of rules and derives a sense of superiority from his certainty that he can outwit anyone. In his opinion, it is not incumbent upon him to put up with the struggles, drudgery, and disappointments that others must endure.

Far from sharing common concerns of his peers, the antisocial child harbors contempt for many of the interests and activities of boys and girls his age. Older youngsters he finds more worthy of emulation, especially those who do not stick close to home and are adventurous. Sandra, convicted as an adult for selling cocaine, reflected that her mother never could fathom why she ran around with older children and shunned most of her classmates. While Sandra's peers were bicycling and playing board games, she was clandestinely trying on makeup and pursuing boys. About her peers, she remarked, "They were playing games I didn't feel like playing. They would get on my nerves with some of the things they did." She disparaged the "Goody Two-Shoes" kids who conformed and were obedient to parents and teachers. As a twelve-year-old, Sandra found sexual experimentation, alcohol consumption, and use of illegal drugs to be far more exciting than doing homework, attending Girl Scout meetings, or practicing a musical instrument.

Gesell refers to the child between five and ten years of

age as "an embryo citizen."[1] The antisocial child does not develop a sense of community or of interdependence. If nine such children were to make up a baseball team, each one would view himself as the captain. The antisocial youngster is not a team player in the sense of sharing and cooperating. His objective is to surpass or undercut everyone else, and he has few compunctions about how he does it. In school, if he is on a committee to undertake a project, he envisions his role as director of the entire enterprise, not as a collaborator. He does not value others' ideas or suggestions or want to share equally in the responsibility for getting the job done. To him cooperation is a form of subordination. While other pupils are sharing ideas and exploring alternatives, he looks on contemptuously and then imposes his wishes. He anticipates that others will acknowledge the superiority of any approach that he advances. Technically, he is a member of a group, but he is not an integral part of it.

Gesell characterizes the evolving relationships between parents and children as follows:

six years: Very sensitive to mother's moods, emotions and tensions

seven years: Child gets on well with mother, likes to do things with her at times. A "we" age for mother and child.

(Boys especially) have long, confidential talks with [father]; think he is wonderful.

eight years: Strong physical and verbal expressions of admiration and affection for mother. Likes father's company.[2]

Gesell was describing a typical process by which a child comes to know the parent in some depth, not just as a gratifier of immediate needs. The antisocial child does not get to know other people as people. Therefore, he rarely appreciates or genuinely cares for another human being. In most interactions, he seems to have an angle, often unannounced. His habit is to evaluate people solely in terms of what he can gain from them. He perceives a parent as a rescuer or an individual from whom he wrests concessions. Otherwise, the parent is regarded as someone who is "on his back"—nagging, interfering, and punishing. Tragically, he never knows his parent as a human being.

As the antisocial child grows older, he may retain a tie to his mother and father, but it is not a strong emotional bond or solid friendship. He desires that his parents remain on call to bail him out of a jam or to provide something that he wants. Some antisocial boys and girls, even when they become adults, have a trace of sentiment for a parent. They recognize that their mom or dad has stood by them, never given up on them, even prayed for them. With tears rolling down his cheeks, one drug dealer sobbed, "I was thinking about my parents, how much they've stuck with me. They'd do anything to keep me busy and out of trouble. They did things for me their parents never did for them." But sentiment does not deter such a person from inflicting additional emotional injury on the people who have cared so much. A frequent response of an antisocial child, when I have talked about how his mother and father have agonized over him, is to blame them. Said one boy with a shrug, "They say I put them through so much the last seven months; they brought it on themselves.''

One thirteen-year-old girl attempted to exclude her family from her life. Never would she bring a friend home or even mention the name of a friend. Yet she would talk for hours on the telephone. She complained to me, ''Every time I'm on the phone, my parents hover over me.'' No child wants a parent monitoring phone conversations, but this girl had totally isolated herself from her family. Her parents could only imagine what she was hiding. It was a classmate who alerted her father, a junior high school teacher, to the fact that she was in trouble. The parents' decision to pry into their daughter's phone conversations had not been arrived at arbitrarily. They had reluctantly concluded that they no longer knew their own offspring. Tragically, this girl pushed away anyone who might have helped her—her parents, school personnel, and me. At sixteen, she became pregnant by a boy who was later convicted of burglary and sent to jail. She finally turned to her parents for help.

A mother remarked to me that she felt that her antisocial son used her ''like a drawer''—pulling her in and out at will. She yearned for a bond with him, but he desired just the opposite—as much psychological distance between them as he could impose.

The antisocial child is unresponsive to others' problems because they are usually irrelevant to his own immediate objectives. There is an imperviousness to the emotional state of others, unless he can take control and be a big shot. I recall a situation in which water started to gush into my office from a broken pipe. An adolescent offender whom I was counseling at the time rose to the occasion. Without hesitation, he grabbed large, unwieldy pieces of furniture, then heavy boxes stored in a closet, and hauled them into another room out of harm's way. I could not have had a more helpful person in the office at the time. Not only was he proud of his display of strength, but he also seemed genuinely pleased that he had done a good deed. Yet this same individual had created disorder and destruction virtually wherever he went without showing a shred of remorse. *It is the lack of personal involvement that makes such a person a loner.* He is ready to be the gallant knight to come to the rescue, the hero in any situation, but rarely is he willing to be encumbered by a relationship unless he can dictate the terms.

Essentially, the antisocial child does not want to put up with other people. To do so requires effort. It demands understanding, tolerating others' idiosyncrasies, working out disagreements, and sometimes capitulating. The antisocial youngster is no more inclined to work at relationships than he is to persevere at difficult academic subjects, for each is outside the range of his interests.

The antisocial youngster has no sense of loyalty to others. To save himself, he will inform on his best "friend." There are innumerable definitions of friendship, usually including statements regarding responsibility, empathy, love, and tolerance in different measures. The relationship of the antisocial child to nearly any other human being fits none of them. The antisocial child's notion of a "friend" is someone who will do what *he* wants. The following episode occurred between two teenagers. When Toby discovered that Bob had stolen a small penknife from him, he confronted him and demanded its return. Emphatically, Bob denied knowing anything about the knife, and a fistfight ensued. Bob tore down the street with Toby in pursuit. They dashed past Bob's best friend, Mel. When Bob screamed to Mel to stop Toby, Mel ignored him. Bob later learned that Mel did not come to his aid because Mel had been in so much trouble himself that he had been warned that one more incident would result in expulsion from a foster home. Bob lambasted Mel and said that if he didn't value their friendship any more than that, the friendship was over; Bob fully expected Mel to jeopardize his own situation to meddle in a matter that had nothing to do with him. No attempt was made to understand why Mel failed to intervene, nor did Bob really care about reasons. So far as he was concerned, Mel had not met his expectations, and this constituted a betrayal. Therefore, he and Mel were through.

If an antisocial child says he trusts someone, it is not necessarily a compliment to that person. Generally, it means that he believes that the "trusted" party either will go along with whatever scheme is at hand or that he won't "snitch" or inform. There is no mutuality in these relationships; there is far more taking than giving. Tom and Pete were virtually inseparable. Because Tom had no other close friends, he clung to Pete despite occasional misgivings. It seemed to him that what Pete wanted to do always took precedence, and that so long as Tom cooperated, everything was fine. If Tom objected to an activity or proposed an alternative, he was ignored or his idea was disparaged until he acquiesced. Tom was so insecure that despite reservations he began "lending" money to Pete just to hang on to the friendship. The one time that Tom balked at making a loan, Pete excoriated him for being selfish after all that Pete had done for him. Tom then resolved to tell his mother what was going on. She helped him realize that Pete had used him and had not been much of a friend. Tom put an end to the relationship by no longer calling Pete and indicated that he was busy the few times Pete phoned him. Frequently, the antisocial youngster will befriend a vulnerable child who has few friends and craves acceptance. Such insecure children may be tyrannized for years and sometimes are exploited financially and sexually. If a friend demonstrates that he has a mind of his own, as Tom eventually did, he is of no further value.

Rarely does the antisocial child express warmth, tenderness, or affection. If he feels it, he is unlikely to show it because he does not want to appear weak. He is sympathetic toward a wounded animal or a handicapped person who does not pose a threat to him. He may be moved to tears by a poignant moment in a film. But in day-to-day interchange with others, the antisocial child is callous.

Children are turned off by unfairness perhaps as much as anything else. The antisocial child cheats, intimidates, bullies, and does whatever he thinks is necessary to gain the upper hand. Through his secretiveness, he loads the dice in his favor so that no one knows what he will do next. The antisocial child simply cannot be counted on. He will give his word in a convincing manner. He will look someone in the eye and solemnly make a promise that either he fails to keep or else had no intention of keeping in the first place. Behind him, he leaves a trail of victims—people who feel betrayed. One mother remarked about her son's lack of friends: "I think they don't want any part of him after the way he has treated some of them." The antisocial person takes no responsibility for the breakup of relationships. If someone discards him as a friend, he is indignant at being unjustly treated. Rarely does he consider what he inflicted upon the other party.

This child remains a stranger to others, even to those who think they know him well. Parents have described their child to me as having a Jekyll-Hyde personality, a dual personality, even a "multiple personality." They live with constant shock waves because the youngster is so often engaged in something unexpected and undesirable. It is unnerving to be living with someone whom you feel is an enigma and generally unpredictable, especially when that someone is your own son or daughter.

As you read this, you may think of antisocial people who seem unlike those I have described. They have families, a circle of friends, colleagues from work, and a host of acquaintances. With their magnetic personalities, they seem to retain the loyalty and affection of other human beings. Gregarious and charming, in no sense do they appear to be loners. The fact is that these individuals are in some ways the most treacherous of all. A researcher who had interviewed in depth several serial killers commented to me that meeting these men at a bar for a beer would be a highly enjoyable experience. He went on to note that some serial killers have dynamic personalities, are highly intelligent, and are great raconteurs. He paused and added that therein lies the fatal flaw. With their charm, they draw people into their web and then destroy them.

There are numerous ways besides killing people by which the antisocial individual who appears to be the life of the party, the friend of one and all, seeks excitement. A man in his twenties whom I interviewed was incarcerated for raping a teenage girl. When he was in school, others perceived him as the all-American boy. He excelled academically, was elected student council president, and participated in athletics. Again, it was a case in which those who thought they knew him well obviously did not. He maintained a façade of respectability, but was able to get away with outrageous behavior on the side. His sexual molestation of children started in junior high school, but was never reported. Not until he committed a violent sex crime did he come to the attention of the authorities. He is an example of a person who was not alone, but was a loner. This man gloried in the fact that for a long time he successfully hid his darker nature from everyone but his victims.

The antisocial youngster is an island unto himself for many other reasons alluded to in the previous chapters. He stands outside the mainstream of society, attempting to impose on the world his view that life is a one-way street. He is oblivious of the injury that he inflicts on others and, in fact, does not even have a concept of injury. When his pursuit of excitement goes awry, he lies and blames others. The result ultimately is that he remains an outsider to human affairs. Toward all the people who believe in him, who recognize his potential, who would like to help him, his attitude is one of disdain. Without effective intervention, the antisocial youngster will remain isolated and see human relationships solely as avenues for conquests and triumphs.

PART III

PARENTAL INTERVENTION: OVERCOMING THE ERRORS THAT PREVENT ACTION

10.

DENIAL

No parent wants to think, even for a moment, that he has a future criminal on his hands. Only retrospectively will a parent say, as one mother did, "My son's criminal career began when he was two." At that time, she believed that his temper tantrums, stealing, and fighting were part of a "phase of development." But now, with her adult son having been convicted of three felonies, she reflected sadly, "It was a phase of development that never ended." I have spoken with parents of confirmed adult criminals who still do not regard their offspring as criminals. A mother of a

125

forty-year-old bank robber still thought of her son as "my baby." To her, criminals were other people who were despicable because they ruthlessly preyed on others and did not care whom they hurt. She didn't consider her son to be in that category.

An article in the *Monitor,* a monthly publication of the American Psychological Association, points out, for example, how essential it is to "take seriously" youthful thefts and not dismiss them as "pranks" or innocuous behavior that a child will outgrow. Identifying a connection between childhood and adult antisocial behavior, psychologists Leah Klungness and Gloria Miller warned that parents must learn to view stealing as serious.

> Researchers have suggested that parents and mental health professionals become concerned if stealing has not subsided by age six, and that a stealer be defined as any child between the ages of six and twelve who is caught or suspected of stealing once every three or four months.[1]

The psychologists stressed that overlooking or deemphasizing a problem such as stealing does a disservice to the child because if it is ignored the pattern is likely to become entrenched and thus more difficult to deal with later.

The psychologists quoted in the *Monitor* article listed several reasons why parents fail to identify stealing as stealing when their own child is involved. One is that mothers and fathers are "not involved enough with the child to accurately observe his or her behavior." A second is that they "may lack effective child management skills." The third reason offered is that "adults may be worried about possible legal or social consequences for the child." Perhaps the most important reason is not even mentioned—a total *denial* that there is genuine cause for concern. Although most parents are quick to condemn stealing, some fail to take the matter seriously when their own child is involved. They reason that all kids do this at one time or another. They may remember sneaking a candy bar or chewing gum out of a store when they were little, and they did not develop into criminals because of it. Even if their child's stealing recurs, they hope that this behavior, like so much else, will disappear of its own accord.

Denial is a psychological defense mechanism that protects us from being overwhelmed by fear or guilt or by a reality that seems too threatening to handle. It is a defense mechanism that can blind us to such an extent that we do not even recognize that a problem exists until it has become so severe that we can no longer escape its consequences. Parents may harbor strong doubts about how their child is developing but suppress them, believing that the wisest course is to endure and let the passage of time and maturation eradicate any potential problems. Many times I have encountered the following scenario. A mother and father consult me about an ''adjustment problem'' their preadolescent is having. The boy constantly gets into scrapes with other children. The teacher reports that he does not pay attention and disrupts the class. At home he is argumentative, disrespectful, and untruthful. The mother, recognizing the presence of a problem that can no longer be ignored, insists on seeking professional help. But the father has a radically different view. He resents being in my office and is certain that his wife is manufacturing a problem where none exists. He takes the position that ''boys will be boys'' and that his son is simply going through a stage. In fact, he may even consider it admirable that his child stands up for himself and refuses to let others push him around. He perceives the boy's argumentativeness as a favorable sign that his son wants to be his own person. Enumerating the many positive characteristics of the child, the father flatly contends that no professional attention is necessary. The mother responds by blaming the father for burying his head in the sand and leaving her to contend with the calls from school as well as with the child's belligerence at home.

Often, as a part of their denial, the parents will attribute the child's misconduct to outside circumstances. They will allege that it is not their offspring who needs to change, but someone else. A parent may blame a teacher or spouse for not knowing how to handle the boy. One parent may contend that if the other were less partial to other family members, the situation would improve dramatically. Parents may truly believe that if their son were placed with a different teacher he would become a good student—overlooking the child's complete rejection of academic work with other teachers in the past. They may think that other youngsters are corrupting their child. A father explained to me that his daughter would take school seriously if it weren't for the weak work ethic of her generation.

In their denial, the parents are focusing on the environment and ignoring the fact that their offspring make their own choices. Such parents fail to recognize that it is the *child* who chooses his friends. One parent may find the other children in the family more fun to be with and appear to favor them, but this is generally because of the unacceptable manner in which the child in question chooses to conduct himself most of the time. It is far easier to be warm, affectionate, and generous toward children who are responsible than it is toward a child who is untrustworthy and hostile. Even if one were to concede that the work ethic is not as strong as it once was, significant numbers of students commit themselves to academic and extracurricular activities and are motivated to achieve. Focusing on negative influences external to the child is harmful. It provides the child with more excuses for his irresponsibility. Furthermore, denial of the fact that the child makes his own set of choices reinforces his belief that he does not have to account to anyone for his decisions.

As another way of denying that their child is exhibiting antisocial habits, parents will often ascribe such behavior to a traumatic event. One mother declared to me that her son was well behaved until she and her husband separated, that he was not a "bad boy" before he became the victim of severe turmoil at home. Two fallacies in her thinking became apparent: first, the boy's antisocial behavior *was* in evidence well before separation was ever contemplated. Second, the other children in the family, who also were affected by the domestic upheaval, managed to go on with their lives without committing illegal acts. Although they too had difficulties in adjusting to the separation, they remained the responsible kids they had always been. Obviously, a traumatic experience may have severe repercussions in a child's life. But children choose to respond to adversity in different ways. A child who is experiencing severe stress from a traumatic incident may become depressed, anxious, withdrawn, or even profoundly disoriented. Does separation, the death of a parent, or some other traumatic event turn an honest, trustworthy child into an irresponsible, dishonest human being? Anything is possible, but I have not seen this kind of development. *Patterns* of antisocial behavior usually are outgrowths of character formation, not products of a specific situation.

Eight-year-old Steve's parents continued to have a bitter relationship more than a year after they had divorced. Never an easy child to manage, Steve had become nearly impossible to handle because of his temper tantrums, lying, and argumentativeness. His father especially seemed paralyzed in disciplining him because he was firmly convinced that his son still was suffering from the trauma of the family breakup which he, the father, had precipitated by having an extramarital affair. At every turn, he would give in to whatever Steve wanted. If Steve smashed a toy in anger, his dad offered to replace it. The father actually had worried about Steve's tantrums before he and his wife separated. But in the aftermath of the divorce, he seemed to attribute all his son's difficulties to the marital breakup and felt paralyzed by guilt from taking any action. He was advised by several therapists to cease indulging Steve's insatiable demands and excusing his sometimes dangerous behavior. Instead of giving in at every turn to Steve, his dad set limits and punished him when he stepped over the line of what he regarded as acceptable behavior. When the father recognized the situation for what it was and took corrective measures, Steve started to improve.

In another common manifestation of denial, perplexed parents become convinced that there are two parts to a child's personality. More than one parent has asked me if his youngster has a split personality. In this form of denial, the parent concludes that the positive aspects of the child's behavior reveal the inner core of the personality and that the negative aspects reflect nothing of the youngster's true nature; they are passing aberrations. A mother nervously said she was uncertain about whether she needed to be in my office at all. She described her daughter, Cindy, as being at times the most charming, helpful, sensitive, and considerate child that anyone could wish for. On the other hand, this same girl could turn into such a belligerent, nasty, deceitful human being that she was unbearable to live with. The mother was certain that the positive aspects of Cindy's personality expressed the "real Cindy." Because of this perception, Cindy's mother believed that the burden for change fell entirely upon her—that she needed to develop the fortitude to "survive" the crises and support whatever positive things her daughter did. It may not appear that this mother was denying anything; in fact, she was. She was doing what many parents do: While trying to accentuate the positive, she was denying the presence of serious problems, hoping that they would vanish. The mother speculated that her daughter was simply overreacting to stress and that a positive approach would diminish the frequency of the stormier moments. I did not concur and tried to help Cindy's mother analyze the true situation. She came to realize that her daughter was pleasant and cooperative only if things went her way. Her dramatic personality changes occurred whenever her mother or anyone else attempted to confront her, limit her activities, or in some way restrict her. She, in fact, manifested the hallmarks of an antisocial personality.

The oppositional attitude, dishonesty, and intimidating outbursts were unlikely to subside on their own or as a result of the mother being positive about unrelated things. Before any corrective action could be taken, the mother had to stop denying that a problem existed.

Some parents exhibit a denial of their children's severely antisocial behavior by writing off the children's rebelliousness as a natural part of growing up. But this is a myth. It is true that some children rebel as they attempt to function independently of their parents. Episodes occur in which they use poor judgment in the way they rebel and, consequently, do things that are irresponsible or, occasionally, against the law. But this is different from the expanding and intensifying patterns of antisocial behavior that I have been describing. To describe a child who habitually steals, lies, fights, and bullies other children as ''rebelling'' is a misconception, for there is nothing against which he is rebelling. Rather, he is on a single-minded campaign to have his way, to gain the upper hand by any means, and to overcome others who oppose him. This child might be more accurately described by others as just plain mean. In short, to consider antisocial behavior a form of rebellion indicates either a failure to recognize or else a denial of the scope and seriousness of the problem.

Denial, if it persists, only exacerbates any problem and makes it more difficult to deal with later, when drastic measures must be taken. Parents do themselves and all their children a disservice when they minimize, ignore, excuse, or otherwise deny manifestations of antisocial behavior. Denial provides the youngster greater latitude to behave in ways that are increasingly destructive to himself and others.

It upsets the entire family, for its members find themselves pitted against one another due to the malevolent machinations of one child. To admit that there is a problem is *not* to acknowledge failure as a parent. Rather, it is a vital, constructive step toward taking the kind of measures that I shall presently recommend, including seeking professional help before the family has been destroyed.

I had counseled Richard's mother for six months. She had consulted me during the winter of a dreadful school year in which this nine-year-old was in constant trouble with his teacher, absolutely dug in his heels and refused to do what she requested at home, and became embroiled in one set of conflicts after another in the neighborhood. Meeting with me just before her family left for a week at the beach, she said that she did not plan to schedule further sessions. Thinking that she was dissatisfied with the counseling, I was surprised when she said, "I have to give you a lot of credit." She stated that Richard's behavior had improved immensely and credited it to my challenging her denial so that she finally saw her son in a realistic way.

"I used to make so many excuses," she remarked. She recalled that she had blamed Richard's disruptive behavior on an alleged learning disability, on his biological father's lack of interest, and on the bad example set by certain neighbor children. "You showed me all that's a lot of crap," she said. "I used to let things go so long, I'd blow up." Whenever she'd start screaming at Richard, his response was to turn her off. Now she was taking a different approach. She noted that if she admonished him in "a low voice, with no emotion," Richard's response was "to straighten up." Having stopped her massive denial of the fact that Richard's choices, not his circumstances, were the problem, his mother found that life for the entire family was improving enormously. I recommended that she call me in September to let me know how Richard was doing because I anticipated problems when school began. When the mother phoned, she decided to schedule additional meetings for herself to obtain suggestions as to how to help her son with school. Things were still going well at home.

Unfortunately, many parents engage in such strong denial that they do not perceive a need to consult anyone until their youngster is knee-deep in criminal behavior. Even then, the denial may persist in some form, and the parents may continue to be fearful and depressed. But if the issue is never faced, nothing changes, and they are certain to be victimized again and again.

11.

TAKING THE EASY WAY OUT— PARENTAL FAILURE TO BE FIRM AND CONSISTENT

As I have already described, the antisocial child's pattern of behavior is to do what is expedient, refuse to struggle toward a constructive goal, and to default on or totally ignore whatever is not to his liking. But the antisocial child is not usually alone in taking the easy way out of a situation. The parent who says yes when he needs to be firm and say no is also taking the easy way out.

Usually, it is much easier to say yes to our children than to say no. By granting their requests, we may avoid arguments, tears, and resentment. Temporarily we spare ourselves and our offspring an unpleasant ordeal, but not without a cost.

Virtually any book on child rearing stresses the importance of firmness and consistency. Parents are told to "dare to discipline."[1] In a book that promises a "relaxed approach to child care," pediatrician Virginia Pomeranz defines discipline as "establishing and enforcing a set of rules to which you expect your child to adhere, in order to make him or her a civilized creature with whom both you and others will be able to live."[2]

The importance of consistency and firmness in child rearing is not new to most readers of this book. However, the consequences of failing to be a firm disciplinarian vary greatly, depending on the child. Some boys and girls who are indulged and rarely hear the word *no* may be spoiled and difficult to live with but nevertheless develop into law-abiding, trustworthy human beings. Other children who are raised permissively, Pomeranz observes, "emerge into adult life with a strong sense of insecurity, of being unloved and uncared for."[3] But this is not to say that they necessarily become antisocial.

My focus is on those parents who take a laissez-faire approach toward raising children who are beginning to exhibit antisocial behavior. Why does such a parent, who is well-intentioned and conscientious, fail to stand up, sometimes against his better judgment, to this type of child? Not recognizing the beginnings of antisocial patterns obviously is a major barrier to taking effective action. But there are other reasons.

Doing things for one's child is natural, part of a nurturing and caring attitude. Sometimes we do things for a child that he should do for himself because it is easier—it consumes less time, we may do it better, and we avoid conflict. Which is easier, putting away his toys yourself or constantly reminding him to clean up after himself? What is easier, nagging your son to make his bed or making it yourself? Which is easier, permitting your daughter to visit a friend after school or insisting that she come home to study for an important test?

Antisocial youngsters have radarlike antennae. They exploit to the hilt the parent who fails to be firm. From an early age, they perceive leniency as a sign that the parent is weak and exploitable. Even a strong parent's resoluteness gets tested to the limit by these youngsters.

One mother was discouraged because she felt that her entire relationship with her son consisted of saying no and imposing restrictions, which resulted in fierce arguments. She had never considered herself inflexible or overbearing, but she was beginning to think she was both. A single parent, this mother despised constantly assuming the role of the heavy, as she termed it. It seemed that light moments in the relationship with her son were few and far between. Yet without her firmness and involvement in her son's life, the boy would have taken more liberties and eventually gotten into serious trouble.

It is hard for a parent who wants his child's love and respect to find himself constantly opposing the child's wishes and having to endure his mounting resentment. It is especially difficult when the parent thinks that he is being tougher than other mothers and fathers and is confronted by his child perpetually complaining that other parents aren't so "mean." It may be true that the parents of the complainer are being stricter than other mothers and fathers. The fact is that some parents can well afford to be more lenient than others, for their children do not take advantage of a situation, no matter how much freedom they are given. In contrast, the antisocial child looks for loopholes even when none are evident and takes license with every millimeter of freedom.

For reasons that are still largely unknown, children differ from a very early age in temperament and personality. Some parents have few moments of serious trouble with their children, while others seem to have terrible difficulty from the time their children are infants. As I have stressed repeatedly, one cannot attribute these early differences entirely to what the parents did or did not do. One mother told me that her son, now in jail, was restless, irritable, and enormously active from the time he was in his crib; he slept fitfully and kept her moving from dawn to dusk. She reflected that he had never had much regard for others. Such a child requires firmness and consistency from the start.

But not all antisocial children are tough to manage so early in life. Only as they enter school and have a larger world in which to operate do the patterns that I have described become recognizable. No matter how much freedom these children are granted, they try to cow their parents into giving them more. A parent under attack may forget that his child is different in personality and has different needs from those of other children who have proven themselves more responsible. The fact is that a child who is truthful about how much homework he has and whether he has done it does not have to be policed the way a child who lies about it does. A child who can be trusted to arrive at an established destination does not require the constant checking required by the child who is devious.

Some parents believe that children should be free spirits. Naïvely, they believe that to impose obligations or requirements will place an unfair burden on their offspring and deprive him of his childhood. But their failure to set limits may have disastrous results. These parents do not realize that a boy or girl who receives little discipline may find it difficult to become self-disciplined. If they have a child with antisocial tendencies, by failing to be firm, they unwittingly afford him greater latitude to do whatever he wants.

Permissiveness does not "cause" antisocial behavior. Different children make different choices in reaction to whatever the environment is. I recall once visiting a relatively permissive open classroom setting where children were independently involved in a variety of individual and group activities, while the teacher worked with one cluster of pupils. Some youngsters were self-disciplined and focused intently on the task at hand. When they completed one assignment, they went on to the next and did not appear distracted by the noise and bustle around them. A few children left their seats for no evident reason, agitated classmates, wandered into the halls, and engaged in horseplay until a teacher reprimanded them. Such exploitation of freedom by the antisocial child is in stark contrast to the responsible use of freedom by most children.

Although permissiveness may occur as a result of indifference or neglect, more often it results from a parent's misjudging the maturity or character of his child. Precisely because the parent believes that his offspring should learn to become responsible for his own behavior, he grants him more freedom than the child is prepared to handle. One mother of a five-year-old decided that she should demonstrate to him her trust in his judgment. She permitted him to play in the neighborhood without telling her specifically where he was going. She thought that she had taught him to watch out for his own safety and that he would benefit from having the opportunity to show he could handle the freedom she had given him. Unknown to her, he was riding his tricycle in the street, playing with fireworks, and roaming blocks away from the house. Like other parents who have consulted me, she had credited her youngster with more common sense and self-discipline than was commensurate with his maturity or judgment. In a sense, she was taking the easy way out: Rather than establishing clear guidelines and supervising her son, she was unintentionally subverting the objective she thought she was fostering—helping him to develop a sense of accountability and responsibility. I am not saying that she "caused" him to be irresponsible. There are youngsters who, once forbidden to do so, would not dream of playing with fireworks, no matter how permissive their parents were. But some others, like this five-year-old, quickly realize when there are no barriers to doing the forbidden and take full advantage of the situation.

Sometimes parents fail to say no because they are so wrapped up in their own commitments and activities that they don't become involved in the details of their child's life. These parents do not meet their child's teachers or his friends; they leave him with sitters and are not a part of the network of parents who discuss and plan neighborhood or school activities. As a result, they may learn what he is really doing only when something disastrous occurs.

Because his mother had to work, fourteen-year-old Dan and his younger brother were left alone on summer days from seven in the morning until five in the afternoon. During the school year, they were unsupervised after school. Dan's mother believed that he was dependable enough to take care of himself and his brother. She was shocked and grief-stricken when Dan was arrested for severely beating a much younger neighborhood child. Burdened as she was with her job and trying as a single parent to run a home, she simply did not know what her son was doing in his free time. I am not suggesting that the mother's leaving Dan alone was the cause of the assault. Many boys and girls are latchkey children, but they do not assault their neighbors. But well before Dan reached adolescence, his mother was so wrapped up in her own marital problems and commitments at work that she had reached a point where she no longer knew her son. My point is that it takes a lot of determination to stay involved in a child's life, especially when there are competing demands.

But it is a necessary part of parenting. Dan's mother did not recognize warning signs that something was wrong. For several years, Dan's interest in school had been fading. His mother took little notice because, until the year before the assault, his report card showed satisfactory grades. She was unaware that these grades had been achieved with minimal effort. She hardly noticed that he had become less communicative about his friends and their activities and that his grades were dropping. Actually, he had developed a whole new group of friends, and he was volunteering next to nothing about them or about where he was going and what he was doing. Several times he had surreptitiously slipped out of the house late at night. His mother knew this, dismissed its importance, and left it to his father (who lived nearby) to punish him. Before the assault, she still thought her son was trustworthy enough to merit the moped he had been nagging her about for months.

Some children seem to be responsible no matter how little their parents are involved in their lives. The antisocial youngster's personality is such that his parents have to be in close touch with his activities virtually all the time. He prefers that they stay out of his life, but that is all the more reason that the parent *must* remain involved.

Some parents take the easy way out because they are reacting to memories of their own upbringing. Remembering how tyrannically strict her parents were, one mother was determined to spare her child the kind of unpleasant experiences that she had endured. So she went to the opposite extreme. Taking a laissez-faire attitude, she rarely disciplined her child, but later felt guilty and angry—and betrayed—when he gained the reputation of the neighborhood nuisance and bully. The opposite also occurs. A parent who rarely experienced firmness and structure as a child himself may identify with his permissive parent and adopt a similar course with his own youngster.

Generally, parents do not surrender their authority to a child intentionally. Against one's better judgment, though, it is often easier to yield to a child's unrelenting pressure than to fight it one more time. It is easy to let children make decisions that a parent should shoulder. Besieged by a difficult, determined child, it is easy for a worn-down mother or father to capitulate reluctantly to a child's demands rather than face a torrent of hostility.

Some parents believe that soliciting a child's opinion binds them to agree with it. The antisocial child knows how to take full advantage of that. He undermines parental attempts to be democratic by converting them into opportunities to pursue his own, often well-concealed agenda. He sulks and says to the parent, "You always ask my opinion, then you do as you want." Desiring both to placate his child and to reduce the unrelieved tension in the air, the parent yields to the child's wishes in another case of successful psychological intimidation.

The antisocial child has an uncanny sense of how to prey upon any uncertainty in the mother or father. Most parents want to be reasonable and to be regarded as reasonable by their children. The antisocial child knows this and tries to make the parent who opposes his wishes feel like an arbitrary dictator. If the parent falls into the trap, he will back down on the issue of the moment, and the child will have his way. If such a child perceives a parent to be uncertain, he seizes upon the indecisiveness and asserts how much nicer, more trusting, and more understanding other parents are. The burden then shifts so that the parent feels he has to prove something to the child. Now the easy way out is for the demoralized parent to feel better temporarily by letting the child have his way: The parent has appeased his conscience and appeased the child. The child considers himself victorious, and it is not long until he resumes his psychological warfare and again tyrannizes his parents.

Letting a child drop out of something worthwhile because he temporarily finds it unpleasant, not verifying that the child has completed his work, making empty threats—all are ways in which parents take the most expedient path, and even set a poor example for their children. Again, the price is paid later. Deciding whether or not to allow a child to drop out of something because he is bored or finds it difficult is a dilemma nearly all of us face at one time or another. But the parent of the antisocial child faces it constantly. That child ignores or defaults on any task he dislikes. He operates with the attitude "If I like it, I'll do it; if not, the heck with it." This can become a way of life, and ever harder to correct as he grows older. The antisocial child will count on the fact that if his parents permit him to drop out of one thing, a precedent is set; he will then be able immediately to drop virtually any activity that he finds difficult or boring.

Children need to know what is expected of them and what the consequences will be if they do something harmful to themselves or others. Even if a parent recognizes that he has a child who is not learning to become responsible, it requires considerable psychological backbone to say no and impose consequences for irresponsible behavior. Few parents like to feel that they are functioning as detectives or policemen. They would much rather give their child room to explore his world and learn by trial and error. But the kind of child I am describing does not benefit from his mistakes because to him they are not mistakes, they are opportunities. His orientation is to figure out ever more ingenious ways to subvert and erode parental authority in order to pursue whatever agenda he wants. With a firm, yet loving hand, parents must establish deterrence to the types of behavior described in the first half of this book. A parent will have to swallow his distaste for frequently saying no and for imposing significant consequences for destructive behavior. What appears to be the easy way out—being uninvolved, capitulating to the child's unreasonable demands, allowing him to drop out of anything he finds disagreeable or boring, denying that a problem exists—all give the child the upper hand and assure more trouble for all concerned down the road. Eventually he will be completely beyond parental control and will perhaps destroy the family unit.

You may wonder at this point whether a parent's cracking down will have an effect opposite to that which is intended. Won't the child become more resentful and determined to outwit or defy the parent? In answering that question, it's important to consider whether the parent takes action early enough, before the behavior becomes extreme. One lady in a town where I was speaking told me of an incident that occurred when her son was three years old. The two of them were in the car, traveling home from shopping. She heard rustling papers and babbling from the backseat where the boy was securely belted into his car seat. At a red light, she turned her head and saw that her son was turning pages of a comic book that she had not purchased. She turned the car and headed back to the store, driving well out of her way. She took her boy into the store, reprimanded him for taking the comic book and instructed him to hand it to the clerk. She explained to her child that people must pay for merchandise, not help themselves. She told me that her son, now age nineteen, never stole again.

Deterrence works for most children. The mother certainly did not cause her child to steal the comic book. But she had a choice about how to handle the incident. She could have ignored it, and he still might never have stolen again. But she did not want to risk it. Rarely can we successfully predict whether a three-year-old is an incipient criminal. If our interest is in preventing antisocial behavior, doing what this mother did can only transmit an essential message early in the child's life. A mother who decides finally to get tough with a fifteen-year-old who has been incorrigible for years may not meet with great success. But even then, it is better that she attempt to be firm and consistent rather than do nothing at all.

A second determinant of a child's response to greater firmness is the manner in which the parent attempts to discipline. I don't wish parents to misinterpret what I am advising: Being firm does not call for being any less loving, and it certainly does not call for harshness or abuse. Parents who equate leniency with love often have unceasing difficulty controlling their children. Life holds consequences for irresponsible and destructive behavior. What could be more loving than to help a child learn this early, when penalties for misbehavior are far less severe than they will be later in life?

Parents may be inclined to be both firm and consistent if they recognize that their child's misbehavior is beginning to fall into a *pattern*. If they perceive misconduct in terms of isolated incidents that bear no relationship to one another, they may react situationally or not at all. How then does one determine that a pattern is emerging that requires some type of consistent parental action?

One suggestion that I have made is for parents to keep a log or diary of events. This is not especially time-consuming, but you have to remember to do it. More than once, I have seen parents who minimized the significance of a particular incident change their approach after they have logged repeated episodes of comparable behavior.

An example is lying. Few parents approve of a child's lying, but they realize that even a child who is usually honest may fail to tell the truth in order to save face. When a teacher calls to find out why a parent did not return a permission form so that his son could go on a field trip, that may be the first time the parent even knew that a field trip was scheduled. Losing a form is hardly a cardinal sin, but a parent is more likely to feel unsettled by the youngster's claiming he never received such a form when he was in school on the day that every child in his class was handed one. Not wanting to overreact, the parent admonishes his son to be more careful the next time and to tell the truth if he loses something; no further thought is given to the matter. However, a series of events in which the child fails to take responsibility and then lies about it should elicit a different response. With the day-to-day swirl of events, parents often don't connect incidents that are similar.

I am not suggesting that parents always anticipate the worst. What is needed is an approach somewhere in between overreacting to a fib and letting a series of lies pass without addressing lying as an issue. If a parent is having doubts about whether an undesirable pattern in any area is in the process of being established, keeping a log of the behavior in question is a good way to monitor and identify it. It becomes easier to be firm and consistent in taking corrective action (without feeling guilty) when a parent has something specific to address, not simply his hazy recollection, his fears, or his imagination.

12.

FAILURE TO DEMAND ACCOUNTABILITY AND TRUSTWORTHINESS

If you had a twenty-four-hour videotape of a day in the life of your child, and you could see everything he was doing, how great a discrepancy would exist between what he has disclosed to you and the unedited picture the tape would reveal? This is the accountability issue. At its heart lies the child's integrity and trustworthiness.

I am not suggesting that it would be desirable to have such a videotape, for that would constitute an abhorrent invasion of a child's privacy. Nor am I suggesting that many adults or children would score 100 percent on a

149

videotape test of accountability that would match one's words with one's recorded actions. All I'm saying is that the parents of a responsible child would have few surprises watching such a hypothetical tape. The less a child has to conceal, the more accountable for his behavior he is willing to be. By accountable, I mean that he would represent his activities as they are.

For most of us, accountability is built into life. A wife trusts her husband on a business trip. If the marriage is sound, he would not hesitate to account for the time he spent away from her. Consider a sales representative who spends each day away from the home office calling on prospective customers. Even though no one checks his every move, his employer has a right to expect that a videotape of any workday would show him devoting his time to marketing the company's product, not napping, carousing in bars, or in other ways wasting the company's time and money. A teenager borrows the family car for an agreed-upon length of time to drive to the library to engage in research. His parents trust him to do just that. They do not expect him to spend most of the time at a friend's house, only to rush to the library at the last minute in order to return home with a few books, thereby giving the impression that he has been engaged in scholarly pursuits.

Needless to say, the more truthfully a person represents or accounts for himself and his activities, the more he merits the trust of others. Parents vary greatly in how accountable they expect their children to be.

I have already pointed out that much of the emphasis in

contemporary psychology holds parents accountable for their children's problems. This is as true in regard to the development of trustworthiness as in anything else. Books on the psychology of child development underscore not only the necessity for the parent to *be* trustworthy, but that he or she must also be *perceived* as trustworthy by the child from infancy onward. Psychologist Erik Erikson wrote that a child's capacity for trust depends on whether he was able to trust those who cared for him in infancy.[1] Parenting books warn of the psychopathological outcomes that characteristically develop when bonds of trust are not established early in life.

The importance of the child's being able to trust his parents is not arguable. But another dimension to the parent-child bond exists, one that I feel has been largely overlooked: namely, that the *parent* must have trust in the child. Trust is not a one-way street, and children, too, must *prove* themselves trustworthy.

Early parental decisions about how much to trust a child are often based on how quickly the child learns from experience. For example, some children can be trusted to leave home appliances alone. Others, who do not yet understand the perils of randomly pushing buttons, flicking switches, and fiddling with knobs, cannot be left alone near those appliances. Some toddlers can be trusted not to run out of the yard and into the street. Others must be watched every minute. The issue of trust arises in the most mundane matters. Some children can be trusted to remember to brush their teeth. Others must be escorted to the sink and supervised. Some children can be counted on to take care of their toys. Others may deliberately break them or hurl them at their siblings.

As a child matures, whether or not he is considered trustworthy increasingly depends on others' assessment of his character. A parent trusts his child to know when tests are scheduled at school and to study for them. When the child brings home a failing grade and explains that he "forgot" that he was having a test, the parent's reaction is determined by his ongoing and perhaps ever-changing perception of his offspring's honesty. In the case of an absentminded, disorganized child, trust may not be involved at all. If he says he forgot about a test, the parent may consider this an unintentional act. However, with a child who despises schoolwork, the motivation for "forgetting" is clearly different. In this instance, the issue of trust is pertinent, for the child has repeatedly and deliberately ignored school assignments and then lied about the reason for his neglect. Another difference is that in failing the test, the first child is motivated to improve. He may welcome help from his parents and teachers and in the future pay closer attention in class. The antisocial child cannot be trusted to learn from the experience. He still doesn't care about tests or, for that matter, any other academic requirements.

We know that it is part of growing up for children to fail to establish priorities, underestimate what it takes to accomplish a task, make decisions without enough facts, and make other errors due to inexperience. When children make innocent mistakes in the process of growing up, this does not shake the foundation of others' trust in them. Until proven wrong again and again, parents tend to give their children the benefit of the doubt.

But parents must really remain alert and involved to know when that line has been crossed. Parents must know their children well to be able to assess how trustworthy (and therefore how accountable) they are. If parents are not deeply involved with all facets of their children's lives, their assumptions about their offspring's trustworthiness may be unrealistic. A parent might give his eleven-year-old some money, allow him to stroll down the boardwalk with a friend, buy a hot dog, and return by a specified time. The boy would come back when expected, enthusiastically relate what he did, voluntarily account for the money, and return the unspent portion. Another child of the same age, however, having spent all the money, might return an hour late and volunteer nothing about what he did. Asked to account for his lateness and expenditures, he might be vague and elusive and, when pressed, offer implausible explanations. It might be easy to let that behavior go unremarked upon. But parents must force themselves, realistically and frequently, to assess their child's integrity in order to decide how much independence he can responsibly handle.

While advising parents of antisocial children, I have seen how difficult they find it to acknowledge that they cannot trust their own children. They are reluctant to do what is most important—to become more involved and supervise more closely nearly everything their child does. Mothers and fathers often are inclined to distrust themselves or each other rather than believe that they cannot trust a son or daughter. As I have said earlier, denial is a powerful defense. One mother told me that she was puzzled by the number of rock tapes that her son had recently accumulated. She knew that she had not purchased the tapes and doubted that her son had had the money to buy them. But rather than think the worst, she allowed herself to be appeased, at least temporarily, by his explanation that he had borrowed some tapes from friends and had collected others by swapping old tapes that she did not know he had. Not until her son was arrested for shoplifting did she even start to acknowledge to herself that he was a thief. In talking with me about it, she compared her coming to terms with that fact to the stages in which a person copes with terminal illness, a topic about which she had been reading. There were denial, anger, depression, and resignation but, in her case, certainly not acceptance.[2] Having earlier talked herself into accepting her son's repeated misrepresentations about where he was going, whom he was with, and what he was doing, she now became skeptical of his every action. "Even if he tells the truth, it doesn't matter," she commented. "He tells the truth just to serve his purpose." Her laissez-faire attitude changed to a resolution not to let him out of her sight without demanding to know where he was going, what his plans were, and when he anticipated returning. As a result, her son took fewer liberties and became more accountable both in regard to his whereabouts and his expenditures.

In a ruthlessly calculating manner, the antisocial child exploits his parents' sincere desire to trust him. At the first suggestion that he is under suspicion, he decides that the best defense is to launch an offensive and vilify his mom or dad for not trusting him. Instead of the child being account-able to the parent, the child attempts to turn the tables to make the parent accountable to *him*. One woman remembers frantically looking in her purses for a twenty-dollar bill that had vanished. Since no one else but her daughter was at home and she had had the money the evening before, she reluctantly reached the conclusion that the girl might know something about the missing money. Tentatively, she asked her daughter if she perhaps had "borrowed" the money. The response was one of outrage. "Don't you trust me?" she screamed indignantly. Quickly the mother backed off, overwhelmed with guilt for even suspecting her daughter of such a thing. She pursued the matter no further, even though she still had no other explanation for the disappearance of the money.

By seizing the offensive, the child succeeds perfectly in diverting the parent from the issue at hand. Rob's mother told him to give the lawn its final mowing of the season. He retorted that if he mowed it now, she would scream at him as she had in August for burning out the grass. But she couldn't remember the incident. Moreover, she felt bad that he was still so wounded by something she had done. Consequently, she didn't press him this time to mow the lawn. It was only much later, in describing this episode to me, that Rob's mother suddenly realized that she had been duped by her son, who knew she was fearful about losing her memory. In fact, what had happened in August was that Rob had carelessly spilled gasoline on the grass because he was angry about doing the chore. The gas ruined a large area of the lawn. He actually was at fault but had twisted it around to make his mother the culprit. "In everything, he plays on my memory, and I'm whipping myself all over the place," his mother acknowledged. In my office, she recognized that in order to get out of work Rob, in his usual fashion, had willfully distorted the facts and made his mother's reactions and her memory the issue.

Time and again, a child like Rob demands to be trusted, but ignores the fact that trust must be earned. The solution? The parent of such a child must forthrightly tell the youngster that he has destroyed whatever trust existed. If necessary, he must review the litany of incidents that have eradicated the trust and not allow the child to pick apart and dispute each one. The parent must then indicate that with a trust rating of zero, the child will have to prove by his behavior that he deserves to be trusted again. Because the child has demonstrated his untrustworthiness, he is to be restricted and will have to *earn* the easing of those restrictions over time. The parent must decide what restrictions are warranted and what privileges should be withdrawn. Parents should attempt to be explicit so as not to be vulnerable later to charges of being vague or arbitrary. Moreover, one-time follow-through is not, in and of itself, grounds for concluding that the child is now trustworthy. New *patterns* must be established.

The matter of how and when to offer positive reinforcement for responsible behavior with this kind of child is complicated. When a youngster does what he has been told, or refrains from doing something forbidden, a natural inclination is to reward him or her with praise. But with the child who is showing antisocial patterns, there are several cautions to observe. One is to remember that these children are skillful manipulators; their motivation for complying with parental expectations may be sinister but hidden. One boy I can recall, for example, made his bed, took out the trash, and became so helpful and agreeable in other ways that his mother was stunned by the apparent transformation. As it turned out, this was a con job. He expected her to become more trusting and therefore more lenient with him—and she was. Lulled into a sense that all was well, his mother heaped praise upon him and gave him a great deal more freedom as well—until she was disillusioned by a call from the boy's teacher. An angel at home, he had been stealing supplies and extorting money from other children at school. Another boy, who seemed to have a similar metamorphosis in attitude and behavior at home, suddenly demanded in exchange for this that his parents buy him an expensive bicycle. Such instances demonstrate a reverse behavior modification occurring: The child modifies his behavior solely to wrest concessions from a parent. Appearing accountable and trustworthy, he has only become more clever at concealing his real motives.

I have three suggestions for parents about offering rewards to a child who, although previously irresponsible, seems to be newly accountable and trustworthy. The first is to express recognition and appreciation freely for the desired behavior. The second is to emphasize how the new behavior differs from the old pattern: "I'm pleased that this time you admitted you didn't get the work done, rather than lying about it as you did last week." Tell him you hope he will make a habit of the new behavior. Finally, in your own mind, be neither unrealistically optimistic or unduly pessimistic—take a "time will tell" approach. And in your momentary state of relief, don't be too hasty in lifting a restriction or restoring a privilege. Wait until the child provides additional evidence that he is trying to make the new behavior a *pattern* rather than simply instituting a temporary change to catch you off guard so that he can exploit you later. Be open, but be attentive, too.

I have known parents of children as young as ten who have become so cynical that they have withdrawn from their child and inwardly have given up on him. This is destructive to the entire family. If the parents cease to hold such a child accountable, it erodes their authority and credibility with their other children as well and usually leads to conflict between the parents. Even parents who have experienced years of frustration with an antisocial child should make the effort to stay involved and communicate with their son or daughter. The parents who stand firm in demanding accountability have a chance of helping their child become responsible.

Let's talk about a success story in which a mother, at what would appear to be a rather late time in her child's life, decided to demand accountability. Mrs. Stone consulted me about her twenty-year-old son, Frank. He had graduated from high school, but only after four different placements were made in an attempt to find the "right" school. Frank's pattern with jobs was erratic as he tired of one after another and never did find one that he kept for longer than a few months. Frank's best friend was a high school dropout who had a lot of money and didn't think any work was worthwhile unless one was self-employed. He and Frank daydreamed about owning their own business. Frank's routine was to sleep until noon, while away the hours with his friend, and avoid his family.

For years, Mrs. Stone had bailed Frank out of difficulties, including recently paying his traffic ticket fines. Finally she and her husband could no longer endure the way Frank was treating them. "He's abusing us," his mother declared to me. When I interviewed Frank, I was not surprised to hear him complain, "My parents don't understand me." He also stated somewhat huffily, "I don't like working for $4.60 an hour," a reference to a restaurant job that he detested. When I spoke with him in confidence about what a videotape of his entire life would show, he revealed thefts of small amounts of money from his parents, shoplifting, smoking marijuana, truancy, cheating on tests, and using the family car without permission. He said that he would like to live in his own apartment, but acknowledged that to support himself, "I don't want to be working all day long." Frank reported that his best friend's parents had thrown in the towel and given their son the $15,000 they had saved for his college education and told him he could live his own life, but not in their home. Frank wished that his parents would do something similar. With considerable irritation, he said that he preferred not to be around the house to endure his parents' complaints. In fact, he found nearly everything about his father and mother intolerable except their "loaning" him money. He declared that he didn't even want to eat at home because "I have a fat family and I don't want to get fat."

When Frank found that I was not especially sympathetic to his complaints, he became less than enthusiastic at the prospect of attending counseling sessions. "No one else but my parents thinks I have a problem," he insisted. Eventually, I reduced the frequency of meeting with him and instead met with Mrs. Stone for a number of sessions. She told me that she knew she needed to do a better job of sticking to her convictions because, again, she was considering bailing Frank out. His car had been sitting on the lot of a repair shop for three weeks. The shop said that unless he picked it up and paid the bill immediately, the vehicle would be towed. Because her son had no money and she did not want him to become even more indebted, Mrs. Stone was tempted to pay the bill. This time, as she put it, her head ruled her heart and she decided the car was Frank's problem, not hers.

In talking with me, Mrs. Stone decided that because Frank was not setting realistic goals, she must. "I can reduce everything to dollars," she said. Mrs. Stone explained that she did not intend to be mercenary, but her son had always lived with every comfort and, as she put it, "hasn't been hungry." Mrs. Stone told Frank that she was not going to subsidize him anymore. Furthermore, she expected him to work, save money, and find his own place to live. Once his mother made it clear that Frank's days on easy street were numbered, he saw no advantage remained to living at home. "I'm going to work so hard in the next eight months," he told me.

Finally, Frank was accountable for his own decisions and for what he had and didn't have in life. No one was going to give him anything he did not earn, and no one was going to accept his excuses for laziness. He saved enough money to pay 50 percent both for a security deposit and the first month's rent on an apartment that he would share with another young worker. Mrs. Stone was somewhat encouraged, but dubious that Frank would make it on his own mainly because, in her opinion, he simply lacked common sense. Frank confided to me that he still smoked marijuana, that he resented the "dirty, cold" contracting work he was doing, and that he saw no need to balance his checking account. Nonetheless, he was confident that he could leave his family and be successful.

One month after her son moved, Mrs. Stone told me that he was asking for a loan to pay overdue bills. "If I don't rescue him, who will?" she asked me. I replied by asking her if Frank should be rescued at all. After some discussion, Mrs. Stone reaffirmed her basic stance, "It's all in Frank's court." By this she meant that he was completely responsible for his own life. Now he had to be accountable to others on a larger scale than ever before—an employer, his landlord, his creditors, and anyone else who had placed their trust in him. Two years later, I happened to see Mrs. Stone and asked her how Frank was doing. She replied that although Frank was by no means a paragon of responsibility, he was still living independently and she had held firm about refusing to solve his self-created problems. Frank had earned her trust sufficiently so that she and her husband occasionally loaned him money. This was done after Frank proved a legitimate need and signed a promissory note that included a payment schedule to which he had been adhering.

Although these steps were taken with a twenty-year-old, the point is that the burden of accountability and trust was shifted to where it should have been years earlier. In the past, Mrs. Stone often felt guilty for not trusting her son, despite his irresponsibility. Thinking that perhaps she had failed him, she often did not hold him accountable for his decisions, but let him drift along in an undesirable rut in which she and her husband supported him, but he did little to help himself. A 180-degree change in her stance resulted in far-reaching changes in him.

13.

PERMITTING THE CHILD TO DIVIDE AND CONQUER

In even the most harmonious families, it's not unusual for parents to differ in their perception and interpretation of a child's behavior. Disagreement over whether a child is studying hard enough, how much allowance to give him, what chores should be required of him, and countless other matters are part of family life. But the more cooperative and conscientious a child is, the more self-motivated, the less reason parents have to argue about how to raise him.

Perhaps all children form an opinion about which parent is the more lenient. When one parent says no, a determined youngster may appeal to the other, whom he regards as a soft touch. If the child does something that he knows is wrong, he may confess to the parent who he thinks will be easier on him before he is found out by the other. Or a child will request something from one parent, knowing full well he would be turned down by the other.

"Why did you tell him he could watch television when I told him he had to mow the lawn first? He'll never learn to be responsible if you keep spoiling him. I'm tired of being the mean one." Comparable words have probably been spoken in most households, with no long-term significance. On the other hand, such an exchange may reflect a fundamental disagreement between spouses about how to raise their child. Sadly, with such a collision of parental egos, the behavior of the child may be completely overlooked.

As you might suspect by now, the child who becomes antisocial counts on his parents to disagree about decisions involving him. This child has a keen sense of which parent he can more easily influence, and he develops a strategy for getting his way that capitalizes on the situation. The child avoids the parent who knows him best and whom he regards as stricter. More than one youngster has told me that his mother is not the one to consult when he wants something because she is around him a lot more, knows too much, and is likely to be tougher.

Because Doug's mother did not work outside the home, she spent far more time with her children than her husband did. She saw ten-year-old Doug becoming more sneaky, untrustworthy, and unruly by the day. On the other hand, Doug's father, who worked long hours, did not see anything about which to be concerned. In the limited time that he spent with his son, he tried to be a pal and do pretty much whatever the boy wanted. Rarely witnessing Doug's nastiness and defiant attitude, he ignored his wife's complaints and repeatedly told her that Doug was just a child and that all kids go through stages. He admonished her for being so suspicious and accused her of *causing* Doug to become a sneak. Not until a teacher requested a conference did Doug's father have a glimmer of an idea that anyone else regarded Doug as a troublemaker. Even the conference failed to shake his contention that nothing was seriously wrong, and he was certain that both his wife and now the teacher were overreacting. Doug's confidence in his power to manage both parents mounted. Certain that he had his father in the palm of his hand, he counted on his dad to take up for him whenever his mother "got on his back."

A child like Doug experiences a sense of triumph whenever parental strife overshadows attention to his misbehavior. A situation may degenerate to the point where what the child did becomes secondary to the parents' warfare with each other over it. (For example, if the mother and father are at odds over whether the teacher was unfair in punishing their boy, the teacher's actions become the focus of their concern rather than the child's disruption of the class.)

An already troublesome situation becomes especially difficult to resolve when parents differ in their assessment of the motives of the child, too. One may ascribe benign intentions to the child, whereas the other parent thinks his spouse is wearing blinders and making excuses for the misconduct. Did the youngster lie calculatingly, or was he truly unaware that his information was wrong? Did he hit his brother maliciously or accidentally? Did he really not hear when he should be home for dinner or did he deliberately stay out until all the other kids had left? The antisocial child often counts on his parents ignoring *what* he did as they battle with each other over *why* he did it.

The antisocial child even exploits parental conflicts that have little or nothing to do with him. Having overheard a stormy argument, the child may consider it time to strike. He may play up to the parent who seems most worn down and vulnerable and then push ahead with a request that, in other circumstances, he knows would be rejected out of hand. The parent who is demoralized may respond positively to a child, even to one who has recently misbehaved. By granting the youngster's request, he feels appreciated and somewhat relieved from the bitter aftermath of the argument with his spouse.

I have seen problem-plagued marriages collapse under the onslaught of the antisocial child who takes advantage of every sign of parental weakness and persistently pits one parent against the other. Mrs. Thomas and her husband had marital problems before Ben was born. Mrs. Thomas was chronically depressed. Her husband seemed to spend most of his life at the office, and his career had demanded so many moves that she felt she never could establish roots. He was so aloof and distant that sometimes her loneliness was worse when he was home than when he was at work. Moreover, Mrs. Thomas felt that no matter how hard she tried, she could not please her husband or persuade him to take her seriously. When trouble began with Ben, their eight-year-old son, it was Mrs. Thomas's lot to deal with it. Events repeatedly occurred that at first appeared to be minor, yet became increasingly disconcerting. Ben seemed to oppose her from early in the morning until bedtime. He'd resist her efforts to roust him out of bed, then would dawdle in his room, pick at his breakfast, and have barely enough time to catch the school bus. This became a harrowing ritual. He became infuriated if she told him to make his bed or place soiled clothes in a hamper. Certain foods, mainly sweets, disappeared from the kitchen, but Ben seemed to know nothing about them. Mrs. Thomas found that appliances had been tampered with and, on occasion, damaged, but Ben denied touching them. The teacher called to ask if Mrs. Thomas had read a note that had been sent home with Ben. Mrs. Thomas had not received the note. And so on. When she brought these matters to her husband's attention, he coldly responded that she was making a big deal out of nothing. Ben became more belligerent toward his mother, refused to do chores, and lied to her about schoolwork. His father merely chided his wife for expecting too much. Already frustrated and angry at her husband for a number of reasons, Mrs. Thomas now was furious. She felt that he was undermining her, even to the point of tacitly fueling Ben's antagonism toward her because he was so hostile himself. This marriage might have been doomed even if Ben had been an easily manageable child or even if the couple had not had children. But the chances for improvement in the marital relationship were virtually eliminated as the two found new turf on which to expand their cold war—Ben's misbehavior.

I was in touch with this family during a seven-year period. Primarily, it was Mrs. Thomas who occasionally would call to inform me of Ben's latest exploits. (She did not expect me to take any particular action, but looked to me for support that she felt her husband still was not giving her.) Her son's antisocial patterns expanded and intensified the older he grew. He rejected out of hand anyone who tried to counsel him. Placement in a special school only provided him with more contemporaries like himself with whom to get into trouble. Feeling completely deserted by her husband, Mrs. Thomas filed a petition of incorrigibility at the juvenile court. As a result of a court worker's involvement, Ben did not flout his mother's authority as wantonly as he had, but he became more devious. Eventually, he stole a car and was confined at the juvenile detention center.

I do not blame Ben's parents for his increasingly antisocial behavior. He made his own choices. Had his mother and father taken a united approach when I first met Ben as a third-grader, one of two things might have happened. He might have continued to misbehave, or he might have found that he had a much smaller arena in which to operate. Also, the deterrence to antisocial activity would have been stronger than it was. Instead of successfully playing one parent against the other, Ben would have encountered an environment that tolerated far less misconduct and consistently enforced consequences.

In a second marriage, the stepparent generally does not have as close an emotional bond with the child as the biological parent does. However, the differences in attitude on the part of each adult toward the antisocial child may be unusually sharp. Mr. and Mrs. Strong had been married only six months before they found their time usurped and emotional energy drained by Mrs. Strong's son, Paul, who was neglecting his homework, failing a subject in school, and lying to them about a variety of matters. A mental health professional might have surmised that Paul's acting up was an adjustment reaction to the marriage. However, this could not have been the case, as Paul had posed academic and other problems well before his mother had decided to remarry. The couple tried to break Paul's poor habits. As punishment for Paul's sneaking out to play with friends and neglecting homework, Mr. and Mrs. Strong placed him on restriction. He was forbidden to watch television, talk on the phone, or leave the house to see his friends. But since both Mr. and Mrs. Strong worked, they were not present to enforce the restrictions, and this was a problem. Suspecting that Paul would violate the restrictions, Mr. Strong took steps to check on him. He phoned the house, noted the position of the television-channel selector dial just before he left for work in the morning, and tried to trap Paul in his deceptive statements. Mrs. Strong became outraged because Mr. Strong's entire relationship to Paul seemed to be more like that of police detective to suspect than that of parent to child. In reaction to her husband's prosecutorial stance, she became Paul's defender and, to some extent, apologist. The marriage was shaken to its core in less than a year. Mr. and Mrs. Strong requested not only that I counsel Paul, but also that I help them resolve their differences over how to manage him. I worked with them for some time before they began to function as a team, discussing and compromising, rather than allowing

Paul to worm his way between them and heighten their discord.

Even solid marriages have ruptured and disintegrated under the pressure of a child who becomes a pro at dividing his parents and capitalizing on their conflicts. The Potters' nine-year-old son's immediate response to any request was to say no. He threw tantrums when he did not get his way, left his work undone at school, and balked at attending church services with the family. Mrs. Potter and her husband had had a happy marriage and had been partners in the best sense of the term. Not that they had agreed on everything, but they had become accustomed to expressing and working out their differences. Disagreement over how to handle their child, however, nearly became the Waterloo of their marriage. Mr. Potter, who rarely gave up on any challenge, had washed his hands of trying to cope with his son and left it to his wife. His disciplined, commonsense approach, which had been instrumental in his own professional success, seemed to be useless in child rearing, at least with this child (though relatively successful with the other). For the first time in their married life, the couple was experiencing seemingly irreconcilable differences. Resentment ran so high that mother and father avoided even speaking to each other about their son. This wall of silence began to have a drastic impact not only on the parents' relationship with each other but also upon their daughter, who received less and less attention.

Unlike the situation with Mr. and Mrs. Thomas, I was able to help the Potters communicate and work together. Several things happened. Mr. Potter virtually ceased making invidious comparisons between his difficult son and his compliant daughter. Instead, he recognized that they were two different children with distinct personalities, each requiring a different approach. This helped diminish his anger so that he could at least talk to the boy and do some things with him rather than ignore him and mentally write him off. When Mrs. Potter saw her husband take an interest in their son and share some lighter moments with him, she stopped feeling that she had to be the sole nurturer and "good guy." The Potters began to share their ideas, not just harp on their disagreements. They functioned more as a team, whereas before they appeared to be polar opposites. The last time that I spoke to Mrs. Potter, she said that the whole family was doing a lot better. She still planned to seek additional professional help for her son after he went to summer camp.

The siblings of the antisocial child usually are casualties of his divide-and-conquer tactics, too. Life at home becomes a nightmare as their parents' time and energy get depleted. Because their mom and dad increasingly focus on the antisocial youngster, the more responsible children often find their needs unmet. There is little joy in these households. Nerves are frayed, and tension hangs in the air. Even a fun-filled activity is likely to be ruined by the antisocial child acting up and the parents quarreling. On occasion, another son or daughter will become the recipient of misdirected hostility that a parent has harbored toward the antisocial child. It's terribly important that parents become aware of how badly their other children may be faring and give those youngsters more attention and support.

Not only does the antisocial child adopt a divide-and-conquer approach to his parents, but he does the same with other family members. He becomes remarkably adroit at playing one sibling against another or aligning a sibling with himself against a parent. A sense of power and of being in control accompanies his maneuvers. This child, who rarely considers the feelings of others, becomes such an astute observer of his parents, brothers, and sisters that in ways hard to believe he masterfully manipulates their behavior and virtually runs the household.

Nine-year-old Carl is missing a favorite stuffed animal. He frantically searches the house for it, but can't find it. Distraught, he asks his parents if they have seen it, which they haven't. His older brother Art knows where the cherished object is, but has no intention of telling. Instead, he volunteers that he saw Ryan, the seven-year-old, sneak it out of the house to take to a friend's. Art knows that this is untrue, but rather than relieve Carl's distress, he relishes the prospect of pitting him against Ryan in the fight that he knows will inevitably occur. He goads Carl into confronting Ryan and urges him to beat up that "sneaky little brat." When the fracas between Ryan and Carl starts, Art encourages each to beat the other to a pulp. When their father appears on the scene, Art plays the role of peacemaker. He tells his dad that he unsuccessfully tried to stop the fight and believes that both boys ought to be severely punished. The next day, the missing stuffed animal mysteriously appears. Carl gets into further trouble for falsely accusing Ryan, and Art denies playing any but the noble role of mediator in the whole episode. In this situation, Art took advantage of Carl's sentimentality over his missing animal, a fierce rivalry between the two brothers, and what he knew would be the consequences of their disobeying the parental injunction against fighting. For his own personal pleasure, Art had orchestrated a set of events that had upset every member of the family.

You might wonder why Art's parents didn't smell a rat. Did they really believe that Art was a total innocent? Actually, they had their suspicions that he might have had something to do with the disappearance of the stuffed animal and even with the intensity of the fight between his two younger brothers. He had been known to take things from family members without asking and then blame others when questioned. But in this situation, they had absolutely no proof that he had done anything wrong. And with a devious boy such as Art, this is what these matters often seem to come down to—having proof. Art came out of this one unscathed. But the parents were more restrained than Art would have liked in punishing the two younger boys for fighting.

Much writing during the past decade has focused on the psychology of how family systems operate. Asked to evaluate the kind of child that I am discussing, a family therapist is likely to say that the problem emanates not from the child, but rather from pathological processes within the family. Instead of regarding deviant behavior as arising from irresponsible choices made by an individual, this approach conceives of deviance "as understandable only within the context of the current family system."[1] The therapeutic intervention is guided not by focusing on the person behaving deviantly, but by developing an understanding of the "family system." The expectation is that "changing the current patterns of behavior among family members" will alter the behavior of the one member who is behaving deviantly.

Watching a mother and father argue over a child's lying, fighting, and stealing, a therapist understandably might speculate that the child's behavior would improve if the parents got along better. But in the case of the antisocial child, such a formulation would be confusing cause with effect. In my experience, psychological maladjustment of the family system does not *cause* a child to be antisocial. In fact, it is the child's antisocial behavior that, in many cases, has disrupted a harmoniously operating family. In families where severe problems existed independently of the youngster's antisocial behavior, the antisocial behavior was not caused by those difficulties, but it did serve to intensify them. In the Thomases' situation, Ben added tremendously to the stress of an already rocky marriage.

Only if parents understand the personality makeup of the antisocial child can they recognize and respond effectively to his maneuvers. They need to know that when a child accuses one parent in front of the other of a "misunderstanding," it often is a tactic calculated to put that parent on the defensive and serves to prod both parents to argue with each other. Parents must realize that this type of child counts on exacerbating the differences between them in order to follow his own, often hidden agenda. Mothers and fathers need to discuss their differences calmly, then face the child united in their response. They must serve notice to him that he will not be permitted to victimize the family by forming divisive alliances in order to further his own self-serving objectives. If the antisocial child successfully capitalizes on differences among family members, it will be he, not his parents, who is the individual either directly or indirectly in charge, and any semblance of a harmonious family life will vanish—for everyone concerned.

14.

THE CHILD
AS VICTIM—
EXCUSES, EXCUSES!

The child who becomes antisocial is a master at offering excuses that sound convincing to parents, teachers, and others who hold him accountable. He aims to persuade others that he is not to blame, but is a victim of circumstance. His explanation after he has done something wrong often sounds plausible, but it has little or nothing to do with the truth. Most parents give their child the benefit of the doubt. Often they will believe an explanation that they would find totally incredible coming from someone other than their own offspring. I find that in dealing with a child who is increasingly showing signs of antisocial behavior, parents will commonly and consistently make three errors:

1. They believe that the version of events the child offers reflects what really happened.
2. They fail to perceive that by presenting himself as a victim, the child is engaging in tactical maneuvers to conceal or justify wrongdoing.
3. They fail to question whether the child truly is a victim or whether he ended up in an adverse situation because of his own misconduct.

The half-dozen situations listed below represent common instances in which parents have made these errors. In each, the child predictably, though not plausibly, asserts that he was in trouble through no fault of his own. Do you recognize yourself or your child in any of them?

1. An eight-year-old boy claims his mother is unfair for keeping him in the house to straighten a very messy room.
2. A nine-year-old boy asserts he had "no other choice" but to fight another child.
3. It is believed that a pupil is failing and misbehaving in school because he is hyperactive and is having trouble learning.
4. A young teenager asserts that he is rebelling because his parents are "too protective" and restrictive.
5. A young man says that he turned to crime because he was severely abused by his alcoholic parents.
6. A youngster contends that he went on a shoplifting

binge because he was bored and had nothing else to
do.

Let's start at the top and really analyze these situations.
Bear in mind that we are talking about youngsters who are
headed for a life of crime, not just boys and girls who are
unpleasant to live with or who get into a bit of mischief.

1. Looking into her son's room, Brad's mother is greeted
by scattered papers, books and records about to fall off
shelves, a surface that is barely recognizable as part of a
desk, and a closet with crumpled clothes dropped on the
floor. She is irate; she warned her son repeatedly that if his
room were not straightened by the weekend, he would have
to remain in the house until the chore was completed. Now
it is Saturday, and she has broken the news to Brad that he
may not play with his friends until the room is neat. Ac-
cusingly, Brad retorts, "You never said I had to do it
today!"—with the emphasis on "today." He rattles on
about all he will miss if he has to stay in. His confronta-
tional response is intended to shift the blame from himself
to his mother, making her the culprit for being mean and
unreasonable.

Let's examine the process at work here. From past experience, Brad knew that his parents expected his room to
be neat, although they certainly did not demand unreasonable fastidiousness on the part of their eight-year-old. When
he took the stance that he was being unfairly victimized, he
was deploying a tactic to shift the focus from what he had
left undone to the deprivation his mother was imposing on

him. Brad knew it was not his mother's fault that the room was in its present disarray. He had heard her warn him repeatedly about cleaning it up by the weekend, even though he chose not to heed that warning. If Brad could shift the focus from himself to his mother's reaction, he figured she might relent and allow him to go out and play.

This scenario is commonplace enough and appears to have nothing to do with the development of antisocial behavior patterns. Children are reprimanded, and they attempt to shift the blame to whatever or whomever is available. But part of maturing is taking responsibility for one's own actions without constantly accusing others and portraying oneself as the victim. The youngster who becomes antisocial habitually turns around any incriminating situation so as to contend that he is the recipient of unfair treatment. Life with him becomes unbearably frustrating because, no matter what the issue, he represents himself as the aggrieved party.

2. Nine-year-old Michael was sent to the principal's office because he had grabbed his classmate Will and kicked him in the stomach. Without remorse, he told the principal bluntly that he regretted only not having kicked the boy "lower." He claimed that he should not have been ejected from the classroom because he was defending himself against Will, who started the trouble. When Michael's mother discussed the incident with her son, Michael stated he was sick of being blamed every time Will acted up. He told her he didn't know why Will hated him and picked on him. Michael's mother consulted me about her son because at home he was becoming increasingly difficult to handle.

She was sympathetic to his problems with Will, however, and she also was indignant that the other boy had not been sent to the principal's office. She asked me at what point it is acceptable for a child "to stop taking it and haul off and slug" his tormentor. When I interviewed Michael, however, I learned that he misrepresented what had happened. Contrary to what he had told both the principal and his mother, he was the victimizer, not the victim. From the first day that Will entered the class as a new student, Michael confided, he had hated Will because the latter had paid attention to a girl whom Michael considered to be his "girl-friend." Michael wasn't at the mercy of Will; he had in fact instigated the trouble by constantly threatening to beat up the other boy. But Michael's mother didn't know this, and she not only remained convinced that he was the victim of this new troublemaker in his class, but she also feared that her son was a victim in other ways. She wondered if Michael was physically aggressive because he had seen his father physically abuse her before they separated. Although it was impossible to prove or disprove such a conjecture, I reminded her that her two other children were easy to get along with and had never resorted to violence to get their way. In dealing with this situation, Michael's mother made three errors in her thinking that prevented her from seeing her son's behavior for what it was and acting accordingly:

1. She did not question Michael's self-serving story.
2. She believed that Michael might be justified in retaliating because he had been a continuous "victim" of Will's tormenting.

3. If Michael did not have enough excuses for his behavior, she was potentially letting him off the hook
further by speculating that he was not responsible for
his violent ways because of the domestic strife he had
witnessed.

I helped Michael's mother understand that the issue is not
the isolated situation but rather the way her son looks at life.
He expects people to operate on his terms, and when they
don't, he lashes out. Michael readily abuses others, but he
will not stand for anyone even calling him a name. Re-
flecting on what I was saying, his mother observed how
Michael felt he had to win in every situation, and he didn't
care how. Gradually, she woke up to the fact that Michael
was remarkably skilled at playing on her sympathies and
she became less inclined to swallow her son's accounts of
himself as a hapless victim of circumstance.

3. In his fourth-grade classroom, Dean was fooling
around instead of completing assignments. What little
homework there was remained undone. His behavior—
passing notes, getting out of his seat, spinning a ruler on the
desk, and talking out at inappropriate times—was increasingly distracting to other students. Dean's parents had taken
him to a psychiatrist who concluded Dean was handicapped
by an "attention-deficit hyperactivity disorder." Due to the
psychiatrist's judgment, Dean's parents and teachers excused a great deal of his misconduct and his poor academic
performance. My assessment of Dean was quite different. I
attributed his major difficulty not to hyperactivity and a

consequent lack of concentration, but to an attitude of "I don't like school." After all, for hours at a time he was able to focus on activities that he found enjoyable, including television and computer games. In addition, he could concentrate for long periods while sketching or drawing. As to the effort that academic subjects require, he said wistfully, "It's too bad you can't learn everything when you're a baby."

I have seen innumerable cases where a child who does not want to do something is excused because he is thought to suffer from a handicap or condition that is not his fault. Many children who are antisocial have been misdiagnosed as hyperactive. Truly hyperactive children are diffuse and random in their activity. Among the features of the "attention-deficit hyperactivity disorder" listed by the American Psychiatric Association are "difficulty sustaining attention in tasks or play activities" and "[engaging] in physically dangerous activities without considering possible consequences (not for the purpose of thrill seeking)."[1] The antisocial child, on the other hand, *is* able to concentrate for long periods on whatever interests him, but he balks at virtually any task that he finds disagreeable. He deliberately seeks out "dangerous activities" because he craves excitement for its own sake. Even having considered possible consequences, he shuts off such considerations long enough to do whatever he chooses at the moment.

Recently, a teenager told me that he had received a grade of B in business law, but had failed all other subjects. This boy's teachers and school counselor surmised he was depressed because he seemed listless and fatigued to the point that he would fall asleep in class, even during tests. Unknown to them, though, he had ample energy to bag groceries at a store, watch hours of television, and cruise around in cars until late at night drinking beer with his friends. Outside the classroom, no one who observed him would have considered this night owl depressed for a moment. Alert and eager to undertake anything that had the promise of being exciting, he was in no frame of mind to sit in classes after each night's carousing. Business Law intrigued him, and the course was not too difficult. The rest of the courses he found dull and refused to bother with.

Some children are afflicted with disabilities that hamper them in their academic and social functioning, but they do not become antisocial. They struggle to overcome their limitations, rather than use them as an excuse for not trying. The antisocial child often is erroneously assumed to have a handicap. He gets a lot of mileage out of being a victim of a condition that he does not have!

4. Sam bitterly complained to me about his parents ''being so protective'' that they were ''watching me like a hawk.'' Claiming that they regularly quizzed him about his friends, he stated, ''I object to some of *their* friends.'' To hear Sam talk, one would believe that he had absolute ogres for parents. But I did not encounter the harsh, oppressive people that Sam described. I found confused, saddened parents who were groping for answers. They related that in the sixth grade, Sam's grades dropped from a B average to Cs and Ds. By the time he was in the eighth grade, he was failing subjects, getting into fights, and experimenting with marijuana. Now a ninth-grader, he had shown no improvement and, after fierce arguments, had run away briefly

several times. This boy who loudly proclaimed, "I need a little bit of freedom" had betrayed at every opportunity the confidence and trust that his parents had placed in him. His parents were not, as he claimed, being overprotective. Rather, out of necessity and sheer desperation, they reluctantly had become extremely restrictive. Sam protested that his mom and dad let his brother and sister get away with "everything." But his siblings had proven themselves trustworthy and did not require the close monitoring that he did. Knowing that Sam was not handling in a responsible manner the freedom that he had been granted, his parents demanded to know each place he was going, when he would return, whom he was with, and what he planned to do.

Make no mistake about it: The antisocial child is a pro at convincing intelligent, sophisticated, compassionate adults that he is a victim of unfair treatment, while giving no clue that he has misbehaved and brought certain consequences upon himself. I have known parents whom counselors accused of being too restrictive, of not "letting go" so that their child could achieve independence commensurate with his age. When the parents had followed the suggestion to loosen the reins, the child became embroiled in more trouble.

5. Experts have cited a causal connection between child abuse and later criminal behavior. One explanation suggests that the child identifies with the abuser and becomes an abuser himself. Another says that, in misplaced rage, the recipient of the abuse later strikes at society. The cause-effect connection between child abuse and crime, especially

violence, now is part of the conventional wisdom about the etiology of criminal behavior. In fact, such thinking is so widely accepted in psychological circles that some examiners are incredulous when a sex offender states that he was *not* abused as a child. I have known several examiners who went beyond this and insisted the offender must be "denying" that he experienced such abuse. This kind of thinking is misleading for a number of reasons. By no means do all children who are abused become antisocial. They have a variety of reactions, including becoming withdrawn, depressed, insecure, and anxious. Many abused children grow up to be responsible adults who are good parents. These are not the people whose names appear in headlines or on the evening news, so we don't hear about them.[2] And too, some delinquents and criminals may fabricate claims that they were abused. They hope that stating they were battered and psychologically damaged during their formative years will mitigate sentences imposed by a judge or jury.

Still another part of the story is rarely disclosed, if it is even uncovered. Consider the case of Jake, nineteen years old, whom I interviewed in a county jail. He indicated that he had become a lawbreaker because his parents had mistreated him. He told me that when he was a child, his alcoholic parents tied him to a bed, beat him, and locked him in a room. When I asked him if his parents treated his five siblings the same way, he replied, "Of course not, they weren't doing what I was doing." Jake's mother remarked that her son's "criminal career" began when he was a toddler. (Naturally, at the time, his mother was not thinking of him as a criminal, but as a child who didn't know any better.) It was then that he walked next door and, upon discovering the house unlocked, helped himself to as many toys as he could stuff into his arms and bring back home. His mother handled this well. She explained to him that what he did was wrong. When the neighbors returned, she took Jake and the toys next door and had him apologize for taking them. Deterrence like this works for most children, but not for Jake. Within a year of this incident, his mother received calls from parents that Jake was tormenting and assaulting their children. Tricycles that did not belong to Jake appeared in front of the house, then two-wheelers. His mother acknowledged that she and her husband, recovering alcoholics for the last five years, regretted not doing many things differently as they raised their children. But she also pointed out that none of the other five children presented the serious problems that Jake did. Not one of Jake's siblings followed a criminal path; ironically, on the other side of the county jail's bars, one of Jake's brothers served as a sheriff's deputy.

I don't defend Jake's parents' behavior in tying him to a bed, locking him in a room, or beating him. I am only pointing out that Jake had something to do with the responses elicited from parents who were already troubled by other problems. Jake's siblings behaved quite differently and therefore were treated differently.

Sometimes a parent of an antisocial child can weather the crises but will lose his composure over something minor. A teenager was arguing with her mother about how to place a bedspread on a bed. The quarrel intensified, and the girl started yelling and cursing. Her mother had already endured years of similar altercations. She prided herself on resolving problems through logic and reasoning, but something inside finally snapped. She grabbed her daughter, shoved her against the wall, and started slapping her. The provocation had become too great.

I am *not* saying that all children who are hit deserve it. But it is important to understand that some children relentlessly abuse their parents to a point that a mother or father acts in a manner greatly out of character. I have known of cases where such a child retaliates by telling an outside party, such as a school counselor, that he has been abused.[3] Social service personnel are called in, and an investigation is launched that can have wide-ranging and damaging effects on the parents. In one such case, a father feared he would lose a security clearance vital to his job. (He didn't; further investigation into the situation exonerated his action.)

6. One teenager told me he shoplifted because he had nothing else to do. He stole items he had funds to pay for. Some of the proceeds of his crimes he gave away or discarded. The fact was, what he stole was considerably less important than the thrill he got from outwitting the store clerks and evading security. He is but one example of children who, after engaging in antisocial acts, present themselves as victims of boredom. It is as though any action is to be overlooked because they have nothing else to do. The antisocial child constantly complains of being bored. But what does he mean by that? All of us have experienced instances of boredom that are limited in du-

ration, such as a boring speech, a boring movie, or a boring lecture. Many people experience tedium on their jobs and in their daily routine. Still, they show up for work and perform satisfactorily. The antisocial youngster experiences boredom in a radically different way: Unless he finds excitement in an activity that gives him a buildup or makes him feel special, he finds life itself boring. One such teenager, just released from a detention center, was living at home with her parents and brother. She was expected to attend school and had to adhere to court-imposed rules of probation. Bored, irritable, and restless, she had this to say about her life:

> I'm not getting along with anyone. I'm a bitch. Nobody helps me. I want to get out [of her home]; they can put me in jail. I'm bored to death. When I was partying [i.e., drinking and using drugs], everything was happening. What straight people do for fun, I'll never know. Straight people—what do they do? If they started partying, they'd freak out. There's nothing I can do straight—not even sew. I can't concentrate. I'm not content with anything. It's not me. I'm an adventurous person. Anything I do more than once is not exciting.

Obviously, this perspective of boredom is quite different from most people's. If adults do not understand what a youngster like this means when he or she complains of being bored, they may conclude that the child is literally a victim of not having enough to occupy his time. In many quarters, professionals have thought that providing more recreational facilities or clubs will stem the rising tide of delinquency. Most of the delinquents whom I have interviewed during the last ten years had abundant recreational opportunities. But having these resources did not change what they sought from life or how they conducted themselves in the world. When bored, the resourceful and responsible child finds something to do that does not create mischief or harm others. He doesn't expect life to be a never-ending roller-coaster ride for thrills and excitement.

It's difficult to avoid being taken in by the antisocial child's presentation of himself as a victim, because he can be extremely persuasive. After all, we all want to believe the best of our children. But the antisocial child is a special case. He is well-practiced and adept at sizing up what people want to hear and then feeding it to them in a convincing manner. Adults who deal with him must train themselves to listen and, at least inwardly, dissect his explanations. They must develop the capacity to detach themselves in order to figure out whether what they are hearing appears to reflect the facts of a situation or whether it constitutes a ploy by the youngster to worm his way out of facing adverse consequences for something that *he* has done.

Instances do occur when a child is treated unfairly. Perhaps he has been reprimanded by a teacher without just cause. Or he may have been mistakenly accused by a neighbor of damaging property. Even if the child is in a predicament not of his own making, a parent should help him assess how he might have avoided getting into it or coped with it better. It might be pointed out, for example, that even if the child is not guilty of the immediate offense, calling the teacher a name did not help his case. Or he might be helped to recognize that because he has damaged neighborhood property in the past he has acquired a bad reputation and, therefore, will continue to be a likely suspect whenever vandalism occurs. He can then be encouraged to behave in such a manner that he can outlive this reputation and acquire a better one.

15.

"IT MUST BE
MY FAULT"

Most of us engage in child rearing with considerable apprehension, believing our child's fate lies in the palms of our hands from the time he is born. Intellectually aware that our children will make their own choices, we still tend to feel at least partially responsible if those choices turn out to be disastrous. Recognizing our mistakes with the first child provides a powerful incentive not to repeat them; instead, we make a new set of mistakes with the next child. Or we're baffled to discover that what was done for one child who seems happy and productive hasn't worked at all for another. We are at a loss when, no matter what we do, we still have a child who seems to be restless, irritable, and destructive. Reproaching ourselves for errors that we know we made or that we imagine we must have made, we often conclude that it must be our fault. If only we could discover the right solution, the child would shape up. The rounds of self-recrimination for doing the wrong thing are unceasing.

In the last section, I pointed out that the child who becomes antisocial habitually claims that his parents are to blame for anything that he finds distressing. If the parent isn't already blaming himself for something that went wrong in his child's life, he definitely will do so after the child repeatedly uses the ploy to deflect responsibility for his actions away from himself. At an early age, this child becomes remarkably adept at heightening his parents' fears that they are not doing the right thing, that they are not being good parents.

Mrs. Ashley was sure that she was the main cause of her eleven-year-old son's problems. She faulted herself for lacking understanding and patience and regretted frequently losing her temper and saying "dreadful things" to Wayne. She thought that Wayne might secretly hate her and be trying to get back at her. Mrs. Ashley focused so much on her own shortcomings that I had to push rather hard to induce her to tell me about her son who, she kept assuring me, was a good boy at heart. Reluctantly and without casting blame on him, she said that Wayne physically tormented his younger siblings, stole from other children, punched classmates who called him names in the face, wrote on furniture at home, and threatened to run away. As we spoke, Mrs. Ashley constantly criticized herself, wondering aloud if she still had the ''unconditional love'' to give that she had read was necessary to raise a child. Tearfully, she said, ''I'm screwing Wayne up.'' Mrs. Ashley noted that when she lost her temper, Wayne sensed how guilty she felt. It was at such critical moments that he would heap invective upon her and declare that it was her fault that he acted the way he did. He claimed that if she would be nicer to him, he would be nicer to her. Having concluded that she had been too harsh, Wayne's mother would be contrite and resolve to become more easygoing. This was precisely what Wayne had counted on.

Psychological blackmail might be considered the specialty of the antisocial child. By playing upon his mother's or father's guilt, he convinces the parent to let him off the hook. Because the parent feels so miserable, the child is spared the full consequences of his actions.

Nine-year-old Rick got into a fight on the playground that might have resulted in severe injury to another boy if Rick had not been pulled off by several pupils. After the school notified his mother, Rick knew he was in serious trouble. When he came home, his mother lit into him. But Rick was ready. He responded by accusing her of not understanding the situation and of always siding with someone else. He wondered whether she even cared that the other boy might have attacked him and hurt him badly. All he was trying to do was defend himself, Rick contended, and now she was blaming him. Hearing this, his mother chastised herself for blaming her son for something that wasn't his fault. Rick had converted her to his point of view. Instead of continuing to castigate him for fighting, she told Rick that the next time the boy bothered him, Rick should let him have it. Then she marched into the principal's office and vigorously defended her son.

Bailing a child out of a jam that he has gotten himself into is a frequent practice of guilt-ridden parents, but it teaches the antisocial child the wrong lesson. By not experiencing the consequences of his actions, he doesn't learn valuable lessons for the future. From his perspective, each time his parents come to his rescue, he has achieved another victory.

I have heard antisocial teenagers and antisocial adults blame their parents for their own behavior, no matter what the parental approach to child rearing was. If the parent was strict, he is accused of being overly punitive and harsh. If he was permissive, he is charged with having no backbone. If he was "democratic" in his child-rearing practices, he is seen as indifferent.

Asserting that a parent does not "understand" is something that probably all of us have done. A boy asks his mother if he can spend the night at a friend's home, and the mother refuses permission. The child's response is "But, Mom, you don't understand." His mother understands all right. She just doesn't give her consent. The word "understand" here really means "agree." The antisocial child uses "You don't understand" as a weapon, as a deliberate tactic to convince others that *he* is reasonable, and they are not. It puts his parents and teachers on the defensive, as well as anyone else who does not comply with his request. That person begins to believe he misunderstood the child when, in fact, no misunderstanding has occurred at all; the adult simply did not agree with what the child proposed.

Even when parents do hold their children accountable for misbehavior and irresponsibility, they frequently harbor the thought that somehow they were at fault. Sometimes it is simply easier to think this way than to accept the fact that their child intentionally and maliciously hurt someone else. I have met parents who figured that a child must have done something wrong not deliberately but perhaps by mistake, or because, on a subconscious level, he was seeking to hurt them.

"Jerry must really be angry at me to cause me so much pain," thought his mother. She reasoned that some deep-seated psychological conflict, perhaps a buried resentment toward her, impelled her ten-year-old to steal. Mrs. Brooks knew that Jerry often stole things he had no use for or pilfered items that she would have bought for him, if only he had asked. So a lack of money or a need for a particular thing had nothing to do with why he stole. Mrs. Brooks had read somewhere that children steal because they feel unloved or crave more attention. Even before reading such explanations, Jerry's mother was inclined to think that her son was expressing anger toward her that perhaps not even he was aware of. For a long time, guilt festered inside her. I talked with Mrs. Brooks at length, and it was clear to me that she was a loving, devoted mother. I explained that the outcome of an action often has nothing to do with the motive behind it. It is hard to describe Mrs. Brooks's relief when she finally accepted that Jerry's stealing had nothing whatsoever to do with her. During our sessions together, Jerry said he loved his mother, and causing her pain was the farthest thing from his mind. What motivated him was the thrill of maneuvering to outsmart people. Stealing was only one way of doing this. Getting away with telling a lie was another triumph, as was watching someone else get nailed for something he did. Jerry gave little thought to the aftermath of what he did. If his mother experienced anguish, that was not his intention, but it never kept him from repeating the behavior that hurt her.

The youngster who gets into trouble may experience no remorse over what he has done, but his parents are apt to both claim responsibility and feel remorse themselves for decisions or actions that they think may have contributed to the problem. When Bill became involved in drugs and was arrested for stealing a car, his parents wrote the judge a letter. In it, they said that a recent move from a small town to the Washington, D.C., area had been a "culture shock" to their son and that, upon reflection, it had been a mistake. They contended that because of the move, Bill had been exposed to and corrupted by a "wild" element that he had not previously encountered. These well-intentioned parents were not denying their son's culpability, but they were shouldering a great deal of the blame for the situation in which the boy found himself. At least temporarily, they were ignoring the fact that they had two other children who were thriving in the new surroundings. Bill had been the least responsible of the three children even before the move. For a long time, his parents had known that they could not trust him as they could the others. The relocation to a large metropolitan area had resulted in more temptations being available, certainly, but each of their other offspring had a full life with school, sports, and extracurricular activities. Bill had never liked school, and it was true he found it easier to skip than he had in his former school. Because both parents were working, he had more time to himself and little supervision. One could conjecture that had the family remained in the small town, this particular youth might have been deterred from criminal activity, but that is by no means certain. Furthermore, it disregards the fact that the move was perhaps advantageous to the family as a whole. Bill's siblings loved being in the Washington area and took advantage of much that it had to offer, and their parents were delighted with their new job opportunities.

If you have a child who is antisocial, you find yourself alone with the problem. It becomes hard to engage in the usual conversation that goes on among parents; it's awkward and embarrassing to talk with others when your child is failing his classes and you know he is disliked for causing trouble in the neighborhood. Even when you are able to brush aside some of the problems and find positive things to say, you know that others are aware of the trouble your child is creating. And deep down, you believe, probably correctly, that others are blaming you for creating a monster. You even fear talking to your own parents about their grandchild, certain that they too will be judgmental and blame you for the youngster's problems. The finger of blame seems to point at you from all directions, reinforcing your own belief that you truly have failed as a parent.

Although I hope I have convinced you otherwise, you may persist in thinking that children become antisocial because of something their parents did or failed to do. Let me leave you with this thought on the subject. As I mentioned at the outset of this book, I am a parent. When I'm asked about my two boys, I reply that they are bringing up my wife and me very well. The differences in their personalities and temperaments have amazed us from their birth. As an article appearing in a popular newspaper magazine put it:

Scientists now know for sure what parents had only suspected. Each baby is born with a temperament unlike that of any other. . . . A baby comes into the world with a distinct personality, ready to respond in his or her individual way to parents and to the environment.[1]

While this may seem hardly a revolutionary concept to parents of more than one child, it is an important one: Individual differences exist from birth. Children *do* in fact bring up parents as well as vice versa.

You might think that I have rejected one extreme position only to take another. Am I now saying it isn't rotten parents who are at fault, but those rotten kids? Am I going even further to imply that some kids are born bad? My response is that neither statement represents my position.

First of all, it is not a matter of casting about for someone to blame. Yes, certainly the offspring of inadequate, uncaring, and abusive parents are likely to suffer. But by no means does it follow that all will become criminals. It is precisely such all-too-simplistic cause-effect connections between environmental conditions and individual choices with which I have taken issue throughout this book. One must rather ask, How does the child choose to deal with the deficiencies of his parents? Many human beings will turn out well despite their parents, not because of them.

Often I am asked if I have concluded that antisocial boys and girls are born that way. I am not adopting that explanation either. We still do not know enough about the causes of human behavior. Certainly, genetic contributions to personality are an important area for continuing scientific inquiry. But because we do not know the cause or causes of something, it is irresponsible to *assume* that genetics holds the key. Even *if* there were a genetic contribution to the formation of the antisocial personality, that would not mean that prison or some other doom invariably would be the individual's destiny. The person still would be faced with a lifetime of making free choices and could be helped to make responsible ones.

The critical question is how does a child deal with either his genetic background, if that is involved, or his environment? With respect to the former, people cope differently with genetic handicaps. Having a genetic predisposition to alcoholism, for example, does not mean that a person will in fact become an alcoholic. He still has the choice of whether or not to drink.

Finally, I am not whitewashing parental insufficiencies or absolving parents of responsibility. We must of course be the best parents we know how to be—loving, nurturing, responsible, emotionally stable, sensitive, consistent—the list goes on and on. But even our possessing all these qualities cannot guarantee that our children will turn out as we hope. We can love, teach, encourage, restrain, praise, and punish, but we cannot make choices *for* our children. That is up to them.

16.

IN CONCLUSION

Throughout this book, I have been talking about a particular kind of child—a child who has an agenda for living that is distinctly different from that of most children, a child with a set of premises about the world that are enormously at odds with those of his more conforming peers. We still do not know the ''root causes'' that make the antisocial child the way he is. But even having those answers would not ensure that the antisocial child would become a responsible human being.

In order to intervene effectively, we must know first with

whom we are dealing. In the first part of this book, I identified the earliest hallmarks of such a child, thus making corrective intervention possible before he becomes a one-man crime wave. I discussed common misconceptions about this type of child held by well-intentioned, conscientious parents and other adults, and why they are harmful to harbor. It's most important that we correct our own thinking errors if we are to have any chance whatsoever of intervening effectively in the lives of children who are on the road to becoming antisocial.

It's equally important to recognize that measures that have worked in parenting, teaching, and counseling children with other problems are not effective with the antisocial child. For example, children riddled with self-doubt about their social or academic competence need a nurturing, encouraging approach and carefully structured opportunities in which they may succeed and thereby develop a better self-image. A child who suffers from paralyzing anxiety may benefit from forms of behavioral conditioning. Withdrawn children need help to perceive in a realistic way the advantages of various kinds of social interaction.

As I have indicated, the antisocial child rarely suffers from such problems. While other children move beyond the egocentricity of early childhood, the antisocial child rejects socializing influences and persists in regarding life as a one-way street. While other children develop a concept of injury to others and learn to empathize, this child deliberately ferrets out others' weaknesses and identifies their vulnerabilities in order to achieve his objectives, not caring at whose expense. Most children become increasingly realistic in their expectations of themselves and others, but the antisocial child's pretensions continue to outstrip his performance and achievements. The responsible child may take an occasional shortcut, but the antisocial child regularly ignores the obligatory, drops out of any activity that he finds disagreeable, and finds excitement in engineering ways to circumvent the requirements of others. The responsible person lies on occasion, but the antisocial youngster shrouds his life in secrecy and lies to the extent that no one really knows him. The responsible child may occasionally blame others for his own errors, but the antisocial child automatically deploys an array of tactics to divest himself of the culpability he deserves. Rarely does this youngster acknowledge any shortcoming or mistake unless he can turn his "confession" into yet another tool to contribute to his own concealed objectives.

Does what I have recommended work? It depends on what one means by "work," and it depends on the child. In helping people make significant and lasting behavioral changes, I have found there rarely are quick or easy solutions. I have no doubt that parents whose child shows signs of becoming antisocial need to have a better understanding of their offspring's thought patterns. Once they have this and have shed their misconceptions, they are in a better position to help that child develop into a responsible human being.

I conclude by quoting a letter from a mother whose child I first interviewed when the boy was ten. As I write this, Rory is in high school. At ten, this child had fantasies of raping young girls and of having sex with his sisters. His mother caught him lingering around the closed doors of his sisters' rooms and peeping through keyholes. He stole food, money, and school supplies and shoplifted. Although he was extremely bright, his grades did not reflect it. In any game or athletic competition, he expected to win or else he refused to participate. In sessions with this very verbal boy, and in separate sessions with his parents, we explored errors in thinking that each made. I helped Rory recognize patterns of thinking that gave rise to his irresponsible conduct and endeavored to teach him ways to deter ''criminal'' thinking. I assisted his parents in recognizing the behavioral manifestations of those patterns and in dealing constructively with his antisocial tactics. This was an extreme case, and each of us had doubts about whether we were making headway during the two years of counseling. But four years after the counseling ended, the boy's mother sent me a letter. She wrote, ''I analyze him so much in my own mind and I like to share my thoughts with someone who knows him and is expert enough to know if my report attests to his progress or not.'' She expressed her conviction that had she not consulted me, her son would have been lost and inevitably would have landed in jail or perhaps have died. Although by no means representing the epitome of moral character, Rory has improved vastly. After two years of never having been caught stealing, he was discovered pilfering food from the school cafeteria and shortly thereafter was apprehended for stealing from lockers. The school suspended him for a week, and his parents placed him on restriction for most of the summer (the thefts having occurred near the end of the school year). Still, the overall direction that he was taking was positive, as his parents noted.

> Rory does seem different emotionally. . . . He—dare I say it—reflects on himself, his past behavior, his desire to control himself. . . . When he failed his science test, he said, "It's my fault and I'll take whatever punishment you want to give me."
> . . . To see humor in some horrible moments seems to indicate a more balanced sense of self—not so rigid, not so egotistical. . . . He may have developed some internalization skills [and] he can now feel and think in ways taught him, but not integrated before this.
>
> I know that our structured home environment has prevented much antisocial behavior. Repeated learning of moral constraints through personal pain now seems to either intrude upon his antisocial thoughts involuntarily, or he has come to rely on them to at least accept the consequences of his actions and possibly stop the antisocial ones before they happen.
>
> If all goes as planned, Rory will graduate next June. He predictably wants to join the Marines. If he goes to college and ROTC, he ultimately would like [law enforcement] work. [It may be a case of] the personality for crime turned moral [that] ends up in criminal justice.
>
> You will never know how much spiritual and emotional support you have given us.

When Rory had first come to me, his parents were feeling overwhelmed—and he was just ten years old! His father had said at that time, "He's controlling our home." His mother, thinking she might have to send him to boarding school, wrote me a note stating, "The sands are always shifting—we are prepared for things to worsen yet hopeful for a favorable tide!"

Clearly, the entire character structure of this boy was not transformed. When he had come to me, his patterns already were extreme. But by counseling him and working with his devoted and very conscientious parents, Rory was helped to make major modifications in what had been expanding and intensifying antisocial patterns. Once his parents became aware both of their son's misconceptions and their own, they were in a position to provide an environment that was loving and conducive to change, but at the same time extremely disciplined and strict.

Rory did not have to leave home, largely owing to the constructive attitude of his mother, who quickly acknowledged, "Both of us have homework to do, he and I." Rory's was an extreme case where the parents took hold, and what appeared to be an unlivable situation improved drastically.

Much work still needs to be done—to identify and help children like Rory, but much earlier, and to develop specific methods of intervention that parents and teachers can use with young children. As I speak throughout the United States, including before a subcommittee of the U.S. Congress,[1] I urge that funding be allocated for research to study children during the preschool years in order to understand even more about the evolution of the patterns that I have described so that successful interventions can be made early. The potential savings to society of such a program are staggering, whether one thinks in terms of children saved from a life of crime; or the tremendous savings in dollars that would have been spent to prosecute and incarcerate these children again and again as they revolved through the criminal justice system; or of many fewer victims of crime.

Parents *can* learn to identify the hallmarks of antisocial behavior before these escalate into full-blown patterns as they did with Rory. My message in this book is that parents do not need to wait to address the problems of early identification and prevention of antisocial behavior. Yes, we certainly can benefit from additional research in our efforts to become more effective. But we know enough *now* to start today to help children who otherwise might be on the road to a criminal career become responsible human beings.

NOTES

INTRODUCTION

1. Ann Landers, *The Washington Post,* May 23, 1988.

1 THE CHILD AS SHAPER OF HIS OWN DESTINY

1. Evan Hunter, *Blackboard Jungle* (New York: Avon, 1976).
2. The U.S. Department of Justice reported in 1980 that the crimes of aggravated assault and robbery "are increasingly becoming the province of youth." Department of Justice, *Reports of the National Juvenile Justice Assessment Centers,* volume 2 (Washington, D.C., 1980), p. 110.
3. Gayle Olson-Raymer, "National Juvenile Justice Policy: Myth or Reality," in *Juvenile Justice Policy,* ed. Scott H. Decker (Beverly Hills, Calif.: Sage Publications), p. 25.

4. By 1985, the administrator of the Office of Juvenile Justice and Delinquency Prevention reported that juveniles accounted for 30 percent of all arrests for serious crime and that sixteen-year-old boys "commit crimes at a higher rate than any other single age group." A.S. Regnery, "Getting Away with Murder," *Policy Review* (Fall, 1985, reprint).

5. National Advisory Committee for Juvenile Justice and Delinquency Prevention, *Serious Juvenile Crime: A Redirected Federal Effort* (Washington, D.C., 1984), p. 7.

6. Dr. David Levy of the New York Institute of Child Guidance is quoted in Henry W. Thurston, *Concerning Juvenile Delinquency* (New York: Columbia University Press, 1942), p. 33.

7. David Elkind, *The Child and Society* (New York: Oxford University Press, 1979), p. 172.

8. Ludwig L. Geismar and Katherine M. Wood, *Family and Delinquency* (New York: Human Sciences Press, 1986), p. 30.

9. A.M. Clarke and A.D.B. Clarke, *Early Experience: Myth and Evidence* (New York: Free Press, 1976), p. 269.

10. M. Rutter, "Parent-Child Separation: Psychological Effects on Children," ibid., p. 180.

11. A psychologist writing in 1983 expressed what for decades has been the conventional wisdom: "Lack of close family ties appears to be the primary factor in most cases of delinquency." A. Lamson, *Psychology of Juvenile Crime* (New York: Human Sciences Press, 1983), p. 20.

12. N. Cameron, *Personality Development and Psychopathology* (Boston: Houghton Mifflin, 1963), p. 657.

13. R. Clark, *Crime in America* (New York: Pocket Books, 1971), p. 41.

2 ANTISOCIAL THOUGHT AND BEHAVIOR—THE EXTREME

1. American Psychiatric Association, *Diagnostic and Statistical Manual of Mental Disorders,* 3rd ed., rev. (Washington, D.C.: American Psychiatric Association, 1980).

2. In an article on the participation of children in the world of drug sales, a judge's view is set forth in the following terms: "Some juveniles are antisocial and are difficult to reach through counseling." See Lynne Duke, "Built-in Pitfalls Hamper the System," *The Washington Post,* July 3, 1988.

3. CBS News, "The Criminal Mind," produced by Jim Jackson on "60 Minutes," February 17, 1977.

4. William C. Berleman, *Juvenile Delinquency Prevention Experiments: A Review and Analysis,* prepared for National Institute for Juvenile Justice and Delinquency Prevention, Office of Juvenile Justice and Delinquency Prevention, U.S. Department of Justice (Washington, D.C.: U.S. Government Printing Office, 1980).

5. The papers presented at the conference are published in John D. Bourchard and Sara N. Bourchard, eds., *Prevention of Delinquent Behavior* (Newbury Park: Sage Publications, 1987). The particular papers referred to here are as follows: Emmy E. Werner, "Vulnerability and Resiliency in Children at Risk for Delinquency: A Longitudinal Study from Birth to Young Adulthood," p. 40. George Spivack and Norma Cianci, "High-Risk Early Behavior Pattern and Later Delinquency," pp. 68–69. Carl F. Jesness, "Early Identification of Delinquent-Prone Children: An Overview," p. 147, p. 156.

6. Lawrence Kohlberg, "From Is to Ought: How to Commit the Naturalistic Fallacy and Get Away with It in the Study of Moral Development," in Theodore Mischel, ed., *Cognitive Development and Epistemology* (New York: Academic Press, 1971), pp. 151–237.

7. Monroe M. Lefkowitz, Leonard D. Eron, Leopold O. Walder, and L. Rowell Huesmann, *Growing Up to Be Violent: A Longitudinal Study of the Development of Aggression* (New York: Pergamon Press, 1977), p. 192.

8. Denis Stott, *Delinquency: The Problem and Its Prevention* (New York: SP Medical & Scientific Books, 1982), p. 152.

3 "LIFE IS A ONE-WAY STREET—MY WAY"

1. Fitzhugh Dodson, *How to Parent* (New York: Signet, 1970), p. 102.
2. Selma Fraiberg, *The Magic Years* (New York: Charles Scribner's Sons, 1959), pp. 134, 214.
3. Arnold Gesell and Frances L. Ilg, *The Child from Five to Ten* (New York: Harper & Bros., 1946).
4. Jean Piaget, *The Moral Judgment of the Child* (New York: The Free Press, 1965).
5. Church states that the young child does not grasp the basic fact that "different perspectives in space, morality, or knowledge give different people very different views of what a situation looks like." Joseph Church, *Understanding Your Child from Birth to Three* (New York: Random House, 1973), p. 199.
6. Committee on Adolescence, Group for the Advancement of Psychiatry, *Normal Adolescence* (New York: Charles Scribner's Sons, 1968), p. 79.

4 DISREGARD OF INJURY TO OTHERS

1. Martin L. Hoffman, "Development of Moral Thought, Feeling, and Behavior," in E. Mavis Hetherington and Ross D. Parke, *Contemporary Readings in Child Psychology* (New York: McGraw-Hill, 1981), p. 371.
2. Robert J. Ringer, *Looking Out for Number One* (New York: Fawcett, 1983).
3. Robert J. Ringer, *Winning Through Intimidation* (New York: Fawcett, 1979).
4. An example is contained in J. W. Drakeford, *Integrity Therapy* (Nashville, Tenn.: Broadman Press, 1967), pp. 31–43.
5. Arnold Gesell and Frances L. Ilg, *The Child from Five to Ten* (New York: Harper & Bros., 1946), p. 196.
6. Selma Fraiberg, *The Magic Years* (New York: Charles Scribner's Sons, 1959), p. 191.

5 UNREALISTIC EXPECTATIONS AND PRETENSIONS

1. Erik H. Erikson, *Childhood and Society* (New York: W.W. Norton, 1950), pp. 194, 208.
2. Psychologist James Carr addressed the issue about whether the motivation behind the quest for leadership is invariably that of the buildup that power offers. He stated that leaders share certain characteristics including "a clear idea of what they want," "a sense of urgency," and a "sense of 'rightness.'" He also said, "They readily accept individual responsibility."

> Power-hungry people *do* occupy high stations in life at times and some abuse their power; but to condemn all leaders on those grounds—including those whose primary motive was to serve or those who simply filled a vacuum left by the less competent or less motivated—is ridiculous.

James G. Carr, "Leadership . . . Is It Always Power-Motivated?," *Pace* (November 1987), p. 17.

6 TAKING THE EASY WAY

1. This quotation is taken from Jacob M. Braude's *Lifetime Speaker's Encyclopedia,* vol. 2 (Englewood Cliffs, N.J.: Prentice-Hall, 1962), p. 733.
2. Bruno Bettelheim, "The Importance of Play," *The Atlantic,* vol. 259 (March 1987), p. 36.
3. Burton White, *The First Three Years of Life* (Englewood Cliffs, N.J.: Prentice-Hall, 1975), p. 203.
4. Ibid., p. 199.
5. Ibid., p. 209.
6. Nicholas Pileggi, *Wiseguy* (New York: Pocket Books, 1985), pp. 13, 15, 36.
7. Courtesy of Ms. Berenice W. Bleedorn, Minneapolis, Minnesota (undated communication).
8. Lee Hockstader, "Ruling Upheld in Disabled Virginia Student Case," *The Washington Post,* May 29, 1985.
9. U.S. Department of Justice, *The Link Between Learning Disabilities and Juvenile Delinquency* (Washington, D.C.: Na-

tional Institute for Juvenile Justice and Delinquency Prevention, 1976), p. 2.

7 LYING AS A WAY OF LIFE

1. L. Joseph Stone and Joseph Church, *Childhood and Adolescence* (New York: Random House, 1968), p. 292.
2. Haim G. Ginott, *Between Parent and Child* (New York: Avon Books, 1969), p. 69.
3. Marvin Silverman and David A. Lustig, *Parent Survival Training* (North Hollywood, Calif.: Wilshire Book Company, 1987), p. 230.
4. Arnold Gesell and Frances L. Ilg, *The Child from Five to Ten* (New York: Harper & Bros., 1946), p. 156.
5. Jean Piaget, *The Moral Judgment of the Child* (New York: The Free Press, 1965), p. 139.
6. Sissela Bok, *Lying: Moral Choice in Public and Private Life* (New York: Pantheon Books, 1978), p. xix.
7. *The Washington Post Magazine,* December 27, 1987, pp. 16–35. There are several articles that relate to the cover item: "1987: The Year of the Big Lie and the medium lie and the little lie and the teeny-weeny lie and . . ."
8. Stone and Church, *Childhood,* p. 293.
9. Piaget, *Moral Judgment of the Child,* p. 196.

8 "IT'S NOT MY FAULT": REFUSING TO BE HELD ACCOUNTABLE

1. Arnold Gesell and Frances L. Ilg, *The Child from Five to Ten* (New York: Harper & Bros., 1946), pp. 184, 210.
2. J.-J. Rousseau, *Emile or Education* (London: J.M. Dent & Sons, 1928), pp. 5, 66, 71.

9 AN ISLAND UNTO HIMSELF

1. Arnold Gesell and Frances L. Ilg, *The Child from Five to Ten* (New York: Harper & Bros., 1946).

2. Ibid., pp. 341, 342, 344.

10 DENIAL

1. Susan Landers, "Youthful Thefts Called No Pranks, No 'Phase,' " A.P.A. *Monitor,* November 1986, p. 17.

11 TAKING THE EASY WAY OUT—PARENTAL FAILURE TO BE FIRM AND CONSISTENT

1. There is a book by this title: James Dobson, *Dare to Discipline* (Wheaton, Ill.: Tyndale House, 1970).
2. Virginia E. Pomeranz, *The First Five Years: A Relaxed Approach to Child Care* (Garden City, N.Y.: Doubleday, 1973), pp. 112, 113.
3. Ibid., p. 713.

12 FAILURE TO DEMAND ACCOUNTABILITY AND TRUSTWORTHINESS

1. Erik H. Erikson, *Childhood and Society* (New York: W. W. Norton, 1950), pp. 219–222.
2. Elisabeth Kübler-Ross, *On Death and Dying* (New York: Macmillan, 1969).

13 PERMITTING THE CHILD TO DIVIDE AND CONQUER

1. Roseann F. Umana, Steven Jay Gross, and Marcia Turner McConville, *Crisis in the Family* (New York: Gardner Press, 1980), pp. 115–118.

14 THE CHILD AS VICTIM—EXCUSES, EXCUSES!

1. American Psychiatric Association, *Diagnostic and Statistical Manual of Mental Disorders,* 3rd ed., rev. (Washington, D.C.: American Psychiatric Association, 1980), pp. 50–53.

2. In a *Newsweek* column, a writer stated, "The general assumption that abused children are destined to become abusers is simply too facile." She contended that there are human beings who were abused as children and are good parents, but they are not considered newsworthy or "dramatically interesting." Alice Johnson, "Breaking Out of a Vicious Circle," *Newsweek,* June 25, 1984, p. 15.

3. One can only imagine the provocation that foster parents experience with delinquent children who are placed with them because the youngsters do not get along with their own parents. Writer Stephen Fried wrote about a Lutheran home in Pennsylvania: "The staff knew all about unsubstantiated charges. They went with the territory in the child care business. Whenever a delinquent child was punished or spanked in a foster home or group home, the kid knew he could threaten child abuse charges and get some attention." Stephen Fried, "Boy Crazy," *Philadelphia,* October 1987, p. 186.

15 "IT MUST BE MY FAULT"

1. Earl Ubell, "When Baby Needs a Therapist," *Parade,* February 14, 1988, pp. 18–20.

16 IN CONCLUSION

1. U.S. Senate, Hearing on Omnibus Anti-Crime Legislation, Monday, May 7, 1984.

INDEX

215